Barbara

Ill Fares the Land

ALSO BY TONY JUDT

Reappraisals: Reflections on the Forgotten Twentieth Century

Postwar: A History of Europe Since 1945

The Politics of Retribution in Europe
(with Jan Gross and István Deák)

The Burden of Responsibility:
Blum, Camus, Aron, and the French Twentieth Century

Language, Nation and State:
Identity Politics in a Multilingual Age
(edited with Denis Lacorne)

A Grand Illusion?: An Essay on Europe

Past Imperfect: French Intellectuals, 1944–1956

Marxism and the French Left:
Studies on Labour and Politics in France 1830–1982

Resistance and Revolution
in Mediterranean Europe 1939–1948

Socialism in Provence 1871–1914:
A Study in the Origins of the Modern French Left

La reconstruction du Parti Socialiste 1921–1926

Ill Fares the Land

TONY JUDT

THE PENGUIN PRESS

NEW YORK

2010

THE PENGUIN PRESS
Published by the Penguin Group
Penguin Group (USA) Inc., 375 Hudson Street, New York, New York 10014, U.S.A. •
Penguin Group (Canada), 90 Eglinton Avenue East, Suite 700, Toronto, Ontario,
Canada M4P 2Y3 (a division of Pearson Penguin Canada Inc.) • Penguin Books Ltd,
80 Strand, London WC2R 0RL, England • Penguin Ireland, 25 St. Stephen's Green,
Dublin 2, Ireland (a division of Penguin Books Ltd) • Penguin Books Australia Ltd,
250 Camberwell Road, Camberwell, Victoria 3124, Australia (a division of Pearson
Australia Group Pty Ltd) • Penguin Books India Pvt Ltd, 11 Community Centre,
Panchsheel Park, New Delhi – 110 017, India • Penguin Group (NZ), 67 Apollo
Drive, Rosedale, North Shore 0632, New Zealand (a division of Pearson New Zealand
Ltd) • Penguin Books (South Africa) (Pty) Ltd, 24 Sturdee Avenue, Rosebank,
Johannesburg 2196, South Africa

Penguin Books Ltd, Registered Offices:
80 Strand, London WC2R 0RL, England

First published in 2010 by The Penguin Press,
a member of Penguin Group (USA) Inc.

ISBN 978-1-59420-276-6

Printed in the United States of America
1   3   5   7   9   10   8   6   4   2

Book design by Claire Naylon Vaccaro

For Daniel & Nicholas

Ill fares the land, to hastening ills a prey,
Where wealth accumulates, and men decay.

Oliver Goldsmith, *The Deserted Village (1770)*

Contents

Acknowledgments

Owing to the unusual circumstances in which this book was written, I have incurred numerous debts which it is a pleasure to record. My former students Zara Burdett and Casey Selwyn served indefatigably as research assistants and transcribers, faithfully recording my thoughts, notes and readings over many months. Clémence Boulouque helped me find and incorporate recent material from the media, and responded untiringly to my inquiries and demands. She was also a superb editor.

But my greatest debt is to Eugene Rusyn. He typed the entire book manuscript in less than eight weeks, taking it down verbatim from my rapid-fire and occasionally indistinct dictation for many hours a day, sometimes working around the clock. He was responsible for locating many of the more arcane citations; but above all, he and I collaborated intimately on the editing of the text—for substance, style and coherence. It is the simple truth that I could not have written this book without him and it is all the better for his contribution.

I am indebted to my friends and staff at the Remarque Institute—Professor Katherine Fleming, Jair Kessler, Jennifer Ren and Maya Jex—who have uncomplainingly adapted to the changes brought about by my deteriorating health. Without their cooperation I would not have had the time or resources to devote to this book. Thanks to my colleagues in the administration of New York University—Chancellor (and former Dean) Richard Foley and Administrative Dean Joe Juliano above all—I have received all the support and encouragement that anyone could hope for.

Not for the first time, I am beholden to Robert Silvers. It was at his suggestion that the lecture I gave on social democracy at NYU in the Fall of 2009 was first transcribed (thanks to the staff of the *New York Review*) and then published in their pages: giving rise to a wholly unanticipated chorus of demands for its expansion into a little book. Sarah Chalfant and Scott Moyers of The Wylie Agency vigorously encouraged this suggestion and The Penguin Press in New York and London was good enough to welcome the project. I hope that they will all be pleased with the result.

In the writing of this book I have benefited hugely from the kindness of strangers, who have written to offer suggestions and criticisms of my writing on these subjects over the years. I could not possibly thank everyone in person, but I hope that for all its inevitable shortcomings the work itself will stand as a token of appreciation.

But my greatest debt is to my family. The burden that I have placed upon them over the past year appears to me quite intolerable, yet they have borne it so lightly that I was able to set aside my concerns and devote myself these past months almost entirely to the business of thinking and writing. Solipsism is the characteristic failing of the professional writer. But in my own case I am especially conscious of the self-indulgence: Jennifer Homans, my wife, has been completing her manuscript on the history of classical ballet while caring for me. My writing has benefited enormously from her love and generosity, now as in years past. That her own book will be published later this year is a tribute to her remarkable character.

My children—Daniel and Nicholas—lead busy adolescent lives. Nevertheless, they have found time to discuss with me the many themes interwoven into these pages. Indeed, it was thanks to our conversations across the dinner table that I first came fully to appreciate just how much today's youth care about the world that we have bequeathed them—and how inadequately we have furnished them with the means to improve it. This book is dedicated to them.

New York,

February 2010

A Guide for the Perplexed

"I cannot help fearing that men may reach a point where they look on every new theory as a danger, every innovation as a toilsome trouble, every social advance as a first step toward revolution, and that they may absolutely refuse to move at all."

—ALEXIS DE TOCQUEVILLE

Something is profoundly wrong with the way we live today. For thirty years we have made a virtue out of the pursuit of material self-interest: indeed, this very pursuit now constitutes whatever remains of our sense of collective purpose. We know what things cost but have no idea what they are worth. We no longer ask of a judicial ruling or a legislative act: is it good? Is it fair? Is it just? Is it right? Will it help bring about a better society or a better world? Those used to be *the* political questions, even if they invited no easy answers. We must learn once again to pose them.

The materialistic and selfish quality of contemporary life is not inherent in the human condition. Much of what appears 'natural' today dates from the 1980s: the obsession with wealth creation, the cult of privatization and the private sector, the growing disparities of rich and poor. And above all, the rhetoric which accompanies these: uncritical admiration for unfettered markets, disdain for the public sector, the delusion of endless growth.

We cannot go on living like this. The little crash of 2008 was a reminder that unregulated capitalism is its own worst enemy: sooner or later it must fall prey to its own excesses and turn again to the state for rescue. But if we do no more than pick up the pieces and carry on as before, we can look forward to greater upheavals in years to come.

And yet we seem unable to conceive of alternatives. This too is something new. Until quite recently, public life in liberal societies was conducted in the shadow of a debate between defenders of 'capitalism' and its critics: usually identified with one or another form of 'socialism'. By the 1970s this debate had lost much of its meaning for both sides; all the same, the 'Left-Right' distinction served a useful purpose. It provided a peg on which to hang critical commentary about contemporary affairs.

On the Left, Marxism was attractive to generations of young people if only because it offered a way to take one's distance from the status quo. Much the same was true of classical conservatism: a well-grounded distaste for over-hasty change gave a home to those reluctant to abandon long-established routines. Today, neither Left nor Right can find their footing.

For thirty years students have been complaining to me that 'it was easy for you': your generation had ideals and ideas, you believed in something, you were able to change things. 'We' (the children of the '80s, the '90s, the 'aughts') have nothing. In many respects my students are right. It *was* easy for us—just as it was easy, at least in this sense, for the generations who came before us. The last time a cohort of young people expressed comparable frustration at the emptiness of their lives and the dispiriting purposelessness of their world was in the 1920s: it is not by chance that historians speak of a 'lost generation'.

If young people today are at a loss, it is not for want of targets. Any conversation with students or schoolchildren will produce a startling checklist of anxieties. Indeed, the rising generation is acutely worried about the world it is to inherit. But accompanying these fears there is a general sentiment of frustration: 'we' know something is wrong and there are many things we don't like. But what can we believe in? What should we do?

This is an ironic reversal of the attitudes of an earlier age. Back in the era of self-assured radical dogma, young people were far from uncertain. The characteristic tone of the '60s was that of overweening confidence: *we* knew just how to fix the world. It was this note of unmerited arrogance that partly accounts for the reactionary backlash that followed; if the Left is to recover its fortunes, some modesty will be in order. All the same, you must be able to name a problem if you wish to solve it.

This book was written for young people on both sides of the Atlantic. American readers may be struck by the frequent references to social democracy. Here in the United States, such references are uncommon. When journalists and commentators advocate public expenditure on social objectives, they are more likely to describe themselves—and be described by their critics—as 'liberals'. But this is confusing. Liberal is a venerable and respectable label and we should all be proud to wear it. But like a well-designed outer coat, it conceals more than it displays.

A liberal is someone who opposes interference in the affairs of others: who is tolerant of dissenting attitudes and unconventional behavior. Liberals have historically favored keeping other people out of our lives, leaving individuals the maximum space in which to live and flourish as they choose. In their extreme form, such attitudes are associated today with self-styled 'libertarians', but the term is largely redundant. Most genuine liberals remain disposed to leave other people alone.

Social democrats, on the other hand, are something of a hybrid. They share with liberals a commitment to cultural and religious tolerance. But in public policy social democrats believe in the possibility and virtue of collective action for the collective good. Like most liberals, social democrats favor progressive taxation in order to pay for public services and other social goods that individuals cannot provide themselves; but whereas many liberals might see such taxation or public provision as a necessary evil, a social democratic vision of the good society entails from the outset a greater role for the state and the public sector.

Understandably, social democracy is a hard sell in the United States. One of my goals is to suggest that government can play an enhanced role in our lives without threatening our liberties— and to argue that, since the state is going to be with us for the foreseeable future, we would do well to think about what sort of a state we want. In any case, much that was best in American legislation and social policy over the course of the 20th century— and that we are now urged to dismantle in the name of efficiency and "less government"—corresponds in practice to what Europeans have called 'social democracy'. Our problem is not what to do; it is how to talk about it.

The European dilemma is somewhat different. Many European countries have long practiced something resembling social democracy: but they have forgotten how to preach it. Social democrats today are defensive and apologetic. Critics who claim that the European model is too expensive or economically inefficient have been allowed to pass unchallenged. And yet, the welfare state is as popular as ever with its beneficiaries: nowhere in Europe is there a constituency for abolishing public health services, ending free or subsidized education or reducing public provision of transport and other essential services.

I want to challenge conventional wisdom on *both* sides of the Atlantic. To be sure, the target has softened considerably. In the early years of this century, the 'Washington consensus' held the field. Everywhere you went there was an economist or 'expert' expounding the virtues of deregulation, the minimal state and low taxation. Anything, it seemed, that the public sector could do private individuals could do better.

The Washington doctrine was everywhere greeted by ideological cheerleaders: from the profiteers of the 'Irish miracle' (the property-bubble boom of the 'Celtic tiger') to the doctrinaire ultra-capitalists of former Communist Europe. Even 'old

Europeans' were swept up in the wake. The EU's free-market project—the so-called 'Lisbon agenda'; the enthusiastic privatization plans of the French and German governments: all bore witness to what its French critics described as the new 'pensée unique'.

Today there has been a partial awakening. To avert national bankruptcies and wholesale banking collapse, governments and central bankers have performed remarkable policy reversals, liberally dispersing public money in pursuit of economic stability and taking failed companies into public control without a second thought. A striking number of free market economists, worshippers at the feet of Milton Friedman and his Chicago colleagues, have lined up to don sackcloth and ashes and swear allegiance to the memory of John Maynard Keynes.

This is all very gratifying. But it hardly constitutes an intellectual revolution. Quite the contrary: as the response of the Obama administration suggests, the reversion to Keynesian economics is but a tactical retreat. Much the same may be said of New Labour, as committed as ever to the private sector in general and the London financial markets in particular. To be sure, one effect of the crisis has been to dampen the ardor of continental Europeans for the 'Anglo-American model'; but the chief beneficiaries have been those same center-right parties once so keen to emulate Washington.

In short, the practical need for strong states and interventionist governments is beyond dispute. But no one is 're-thinking' the state. There remains a marked reluctance to defend the public sector on grounds of collective interest or principle. It is striking that in a series of European elections following the financial meltdown, social democratic parties consistently did badly; notwithstanding the collapse of the market, they proved conspicuously unable to rise to the occasion.

If it is to be taken seriously again, the Left must find its voice. There is much to be angry about: growing inequalities of wealth and opportunity; injustices of class and caste; economic exploitation at home and abroad; corruption and money and privilege occluding the arteries of democracy. But it will no longer suffice to identify the shortcomings of 'the system' and then retreat, Pilate-like: indifferent to consequences. The irresponsible rhetorical grandstanding of decades past did not serve the Left well.

We have entered an age of insecurity—economic insecurity, physical insecurity, political insecurity. The fact that we are largely unaware of this is small comfort: few in 1914 predicted the utter collapse of their world and the economic and political catastrophes that followed. Insecurity breeds fear. And fear—fear of change, fear of decline, fear of strangers and an unfamiliar world—is corroding the trust and interdependence on which civil societies rest.

All change is disruptive. We have seen that the specter of terrorism is enough to cast stable democracies into turmoil. Climate change will have even more dramatic consequences. Men and women will be thrown back upon the resources of the state. They will look to their political leaders and representatives to protect them: open societies will once again be urged to close in upon themselves, sacrificing freedom for 'security'. The choice will no longer be between the state and the market, but between two sorts of state. It is thus incumbent upon us to reconceive the role of government. If we do not, others will.

The arguments that follow were first outlined in an essay I contributed to the *New York Review of Books* in December 2009. Following the publication of that essay, I received many interesting comments and suggestions. Among them was a thoughtful critique from a young colleague. "What is most striking", she wrote, "about what you say is not so much the substance but the form: you speak of being angry at our political quiescence; you write of the need to dissent from our economically-driven way of thinking, the urgency of a return to an ethically informed public conversation. No one talks like this any more." Hence this book.

CHAPTER ONE

The Way We Live Now

*"To see what is in front of one's nose
needs a constant struggle."*

—GEORGE ORWELL

All around us we see a level of individual wealth unequaled since the early years of the 20th century. Conspicuous consumption of redundant consumer goods—houses, jewelry, cars, clothing, tech toys—has greatly expanded over the past generation. In the US, the UK and a handful of other countries, financial transactions have displaced the production of goods or services as the source of private fortunes, distorting the value we place upon different kinds of economic activity. The wealthy, like the poor, have always been with us. But relative to everyone else, they are today wealthier and more conspicuous than at any time in living memory. Private privilege is easy to understand and describe. It is rather harder to convey the depths of public squalor into which we have fallen.

PRIVATE AFFLUENCE, PUBLIC SQUALOR

"No society can surely be flourishing and happy,
of which the far greater part of the members are
poor and miserable."

—ADAM SMITH

Poverty is an abstraction, even for the poor. But the symptoms of collective impoverishment are all about us. Broken highways, bankrupt cities, collapsing bridges, failed schools, the unemployed, the underpaid and the uninsured: all suggest a collective failure of will. These shortcomings are so endemic that we no longer know how to talk about what is wrong, much less set about repairing it. And yet something is seriously amiss. Even as the US budgets tens of billions of dollars on a futile military campaign in Afghanistan, we fret nervously at the implications of any increase in public spending on social services or infrastructure.

To understand the depths to which we have fallen, we must first appreciate the scale of the changes that have overtaken us. From the late 19th century until the 1970s, the advanced societies of the West were all becoming less unequal. Thanks to progressive taxation, government subsidies for the poor, the provision of social services and guarantees against acute misfortune, modern democracies were shedding extremes of wealth and poverty.

To be sure, great differences remained. The essentially egalitarian countries of Scandinavia and the considerably more diverse societies of southern Europe remained distinctive; and the English-speaking lands of the Atlantic world and the British Empire continued to reflect long-standing class distinctions. But each in its own way was affected by the growing intolerance of immoderate inequality, initiating public provision to compensate for private inadequacy.

Over the past thirty years we have thrown all this away. To be sure, "we" varies with country. The greatest extremes of private privilege and public indifference have resurfaced in the US and the UK: epicenters of enthusiasm for deregulated market capitalism. Although countries as far apart as New Zealand and Denmark, France and Brazil have expressed periodic interest, none has matched Britain or the United States in their unwavering thirty-year commitment to the unraveling of decades of social legislation and economic oversight.

In 2005, 21.2 percent of US national income accrued to just 1 percent of earners. Contrast 1968, when the CEO of General Motors took home, in pay and benefits, about sixty-six times the amount paid to a typical GM worker. Today the CEO of Wal-Mart earns nine hundred times the wages of his average employee. Indeed, the wealth of the Wal-Mart founders' family that year was estimated at about the same ($90 billion) as that of the bottom 40 percent of the US population: 120 million people.

The UK too is now more unequal—in incomes, wealth, health, education and life chances—than at any time since the 1920s. There are more poor children in the UK than in any other country of the European Union. Since 1973, inequality in take-home pay increased more in the UK than anywhere except the US. Most of the new jobs created in Britain in the years 1977-2007 were either at the very high or the very low end of the pay scale.

The consequences are clear. There has been a collapse in intergenerational mobility: in contrast to their parents and grandparents, children today in the UK as in the US have very little expectation of improving upon the condition into which they were born. The poor stay poor. Economic disadvantage for the overwhelming majority translates into ill health, missed educational opportunity and—increasingly—the familiar symptoms of depression: alcoholism, obesity, gambling and minor

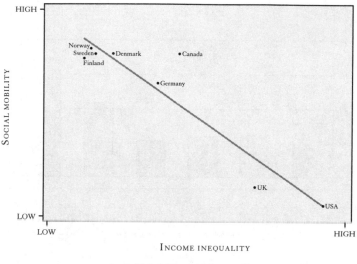

Social Mobility and Inequality.

(From Wilkinson & Pickett, *The Spirit Level*, Figure 12.1, p. 160)

criminality. The unemployed or underemployed lose such skills as they have acquired and become chronically superfluous to the economy. Anxiety and stress, not to mention illness and early death, frequently follow.

Income disparity exacerbates the problems. Thus the incidence of mental illness correlates closely to income in the US and the UK, whereas the two indices are quite unrelated in all continental European countries. Even trust, the faith we have in our fellow citizens, corresponds negatively with differences in income: between 1983 and 2001, mistrustfulness increased markedly in the US, the UK and Ireland—three countries in

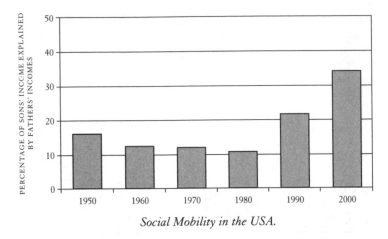

Social Mobility in the USA.

(From Wilkinson & Pickett, *The Spirit Level*, Figure 12.2, p. 161)

which the dogma of unregulated individual self-interest was most assiduously applied to public policy. In no other country was a comparable increase in mutual mistrust to be found.

Even *within* individual countries, inequality plays a crucial role in shaping peoples' lives. In the United States, for example, your chances of living a long and healthy life closely track your income: residents of wealthy districts can expect to live longer and better. Young women in poorer states of the US are more likely to become pregnant in their teenage years—and their babies are less likely to survive—than their peers in wealthier states. In the same way, a child from a disfavored district has a higher chance of dropping out of high school than if his parents have a steady mid-range income and live in a prosperous part

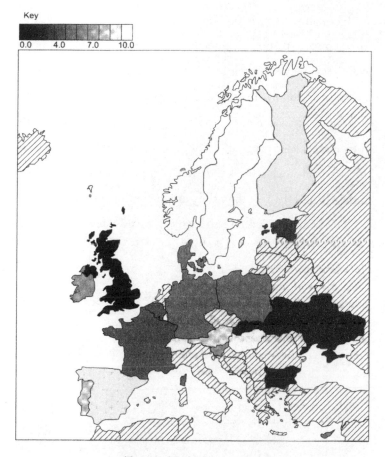

Key

0.0   4.0   7.0   10.0

Trust and Belonging in Europe.

(From Tim Jackson, *Prosperity Without Growth: Economics for a Finite Planet* [London: Earthscan, 2009], Figure 9.1, p. 145)

of the country. As for the children of the poor who remain in school: they will do worse, achieve lower scores and obtain less fulfilling and lower paid employment.

Inequality, then, is not just unattractive in itself; it clearly corresponds to pathological social problems that we cannot hope to address unless we attend to their underlying cause. There is a reason why infant mortality, life expectancy, criminality, the prison population, mental illness, unemployment, obesity, malnutrition, teenage pregnancy, illegal drug use, economic insecurity, personal indebtedness and anxiety are so much more marked in the US and the UK than they are in continental Europe.

The wider the spread between the wealthy few and the im-

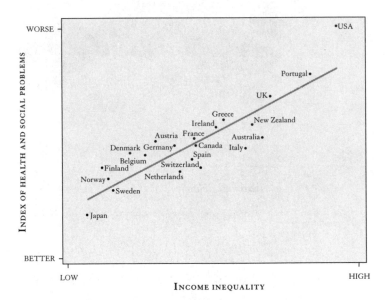

Inequality and Ill Health.

(From Jackson, *Prosperity Without Growth,* Figure 9.2, p. 155)

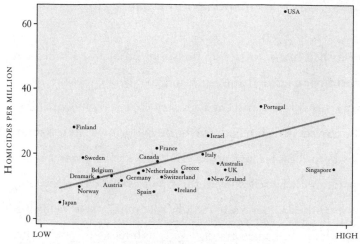

Inequality and Crime.

(From Wilkinson & Pickett, *The Spirit Level*, Figure 10.2, p. 135)

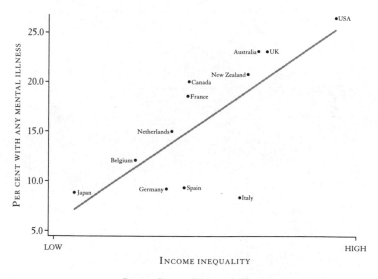

Inequality and Mental Illness.

(From Wilkinson & Pickett, *The Spirit Level*, Figure 5.1, p. 67)

poverished many, the worse the social problems: a statement which appears to be true for rich and poor countries alike. What matters is not how affluent a country is but how unequal it is. Thus Sweden, or Finland, two of the world's wealthiest countries by per capita income or GDP, have a very narrow gap separating their richest from their poorest citizens—and they consistently lead the world in indices of measurable wellbeing. Conversely, the United States, despite its huge aggregate wealth, always comes low on such measures. We spend vast sums on healthcare, but life expectancy in the US remains below Bosnia and just above Albania.

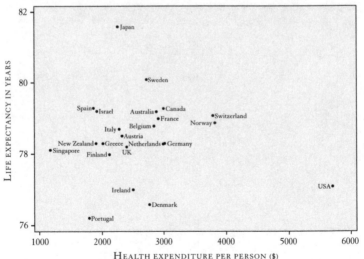

Health Expenditure and Life Expectancy.

(From Wilkinson & Pickett, *The Spirit Level*, Figure 6.2, p. 80)

Inequality is corrosive. It rots societies from within. The impact of material differences takes a while to show up: but in due course competition for status and goods increases; people feel a growing sense of superiority (or inferiority) based on their possessions; prejudice towards those on the lower ranks of the social ladder hardens; crime spikes and the pathologies of social disadvantage become ever more marked. The legacy of un-regulated wealth creation is bitter indeed.[1]

CORRUPTED SENTIMENTS

"There are no conditions of life to which a man cannot get accustomed, especially if he sees them accepted by everyone around him."

—LEV TOLSTOY, *ANNA KARENINA*

During the long decades of 'equalization', the idea that such improvements could be sustained became common-place. Reductions in inequality are self-confirming: the more equal we get, the more equal we believe it is possible to be. Conversely, thirty years of growing *inequality* have convinced the

---

1 The best recent statement of this argument comes in Richard Wilkinson and Kate Pickett, *The Spirit Level: Why More Equal Societies Almost Always Do Better* (London: Allen Lane, 2009). I am indebted to them for much of the material in this section.

English and Americans in particular that this is a natural condition of life about which we can do little.

To the extent that we do speak of alleviating social ills, we suppose economic 'growth' to be sufficient: the diffusion of prosperity and privilege will flow naturally from an increase in the cake. Sadly, all the evidence suggests the contrary. Whereas in hard times we are more likely to accept redistribution as both necessary and possible, in an age of affluence economic growth typically privileges the few while accentuating the relative disadvantage of the many.

We are often blind to this: an overall increase in aggregate wealth camouflages distributive disparities. This problem is familiar from the development of backward societies—economic growth benefits everyone but disproportionately serves a tiny minority positioned to exploit it. Contemporary China or India illustrate the point. But that the United States, a fully developed economy, should have a 'Gini coefficient' (the conventional measure of the gap separating rich and poor) almost identical to that of China is remarkable.

It is one thing to dwell amongst inequality and its pathologies; it is quite another to revel in them. There is everywhere a striking propensity to admire great wealth and accord it celebrity status ('Lifestyles of the Rich and Famous'). We have been here before: back in the 18th century, Adam Smith—the founding father of classical economics—observed the same disposition among his contemporaries: "The great mob of mankind are the admirers and worshippers, and, what may seem more extraordinary, most frequently the disinterested admirers and worshippers, of wealth and greatness."[2]

For Smith, this uncritical adulation of wealth for its own sake was not merely unattractive. It was also a potentially destructive feature of a modern commercial economy, one that might in the course of time undermine the very qualities which capitalism, in his eyes, needed to sustain and nourish: "The disposition to admire, and almost to worship, the rich and the powerful, and to despise, or, at least, to neglect, persons of poor and mean condition . . . [is] . . . the great and most universal cause of the corruption of our moral sentiments."[3]

Our moral sentiments have indeed been corrupted. We have become insensible to the human costs of apparently rational social policies, especially when we are advised that they will contribute to overall prosperity and thus—implicitly—to our separate interests. Consider the 1996 "Personal Responsibility and Work Opportunity Act" (a revealingly Orwellian label), the Clinton-era legislation that sought to gut welfare provision

2 Adam Smith, *The Theory of Moral Sentiments* (Mineola, NY: Dover Publication Classics, 2006, original publication 1759), p. 59.
3 Ibid., p. 58.

here in the US. The stated purpose of this Act was to shrink the nation's welfare rolls. This was to be achieved by withholding welfare from anyone who had failed to seek (and, if successful, accept) paid employment. Because an employer could thus hope to attract workers at almost any wage he offered—they could not decline a job, however distasteful, without risking exclusion from welfare benefits—not only were the numbers on welfare considerably reduced but wages and business costs fell too.

Moreover, welfare acquired an explicit stigma. To be a recipient of public aid, whether in the form of child support, food stamps or unemployment benefits, was a mark of Cain: a sign of personal failure, evidence that one had somehow fallen through the cracks of society. In the contemporary United States, at a time of growing unemployment, a jobless man or woman is thus stigmatized: they are not quite a full member of the community. Even in social democratic Norway, the 1991 Social Services Act entitled local authorities to impose comparable work requirements on anyone applying for welfare.

The terms of this legislation should put us in mind of a previous Act, passed in England nearly two hundred years earlier: the New Poor Law of 1834. The provisions of this law are familiar to us, thanks to Charles Dickens's depiction of its workings in *Oliver Twist*. When Noah Claypole famously sneers at little Oliver, calling him "Work'us" ("Workhouse"), he is implying, for 1838, precisely what we convey today when we speak disparagingly of "welfare queens".

The New Poor Law was an outrage. It obliged the indigent and the unemployed to choose between work at any wage, however low, and the humiliation of the workhouse. Here, as in other forms of 19th-century public assistance (still thought of and described as "charity"), the level of aid and support was calibrated so as to be less appealing than the worst available alternative. The Law drew on contemporary economic theories that denied the very possibility of unemployment in an efficient market: if wages fell low enough and there was no attractive alternative to work, everyone would eventually find a job.

For the next 150 years, reformers strove to abolish such demeaning practices. In due course, the New Poor Law and its foreign analogues were succeeded by the public provision of assistance as a matter of *right*. Workless citizens were no longer deemed any the less deserving for the misfortune of unemployment; they would not be penalized for their condition nor would implicit aspersions be cast upon their good standing as members of society. More than anything else, the welfare states of the mid-20th century established the profound *indecency* of defining civic status as a function of economic good fortune.

Instead, the ethic of Victorian voluntarism and punitive eligibility criteria was replaced by universal social provision, albeit varying considerably from country to country. The inability to work or to find work, far from being stigmatized, was now treated as a condition of occasional but by no means dishonorable dependence upon one's fellow citizens. Needs and rights were accorded special respect and the idea that unemployment was the product of bad character or insufficient effort was put to rest.

Today we have reverted to the attitudes of our early Victorian forebears. Once again, we believe exclusively in incentives, "effort" and reward—together with penalties for inadequacy. To hear Bill Clinton or Margaret Thatcher explain it, making welfare universally available to all who need it would be foolish. If workers are not desperate, why should they work? If the state pays people to be idle, what incentive do they have to seek out paid employment? We have reverted to the hard, cold world of Enlightened economic rationality, first and best expressed in *The Fable of the Bees*, Bernard Mandeville's 1732 essay on political economy. Workers, in Mandeville's view, "have nothing to stir them up to be serviceable but their wants, which it is prudence to relieve but folly to cure". Tony Blair could not have said it better.

Welfare 'reforms' have revived the dreaded 'means test'. As readers of George Orwell will recall, the indigent in Depression-era England could only apply for poor relief once the authorities had established—by means of intrusive inquiry—that they had exhausted their own resources. A similar test was applied to the unemployed in 1930s America. Malcolm X, in his memoirs, recalls the officials who "checked up" on his family: "[T]he monthly Welfare check was their pass. They acted as if they owned us. As much as my mother would have liked to, she couldn't keep them out. ...We couldn't understand why, if the state was willing to give us packages of meat, sacks of potatoes and fruit, and cans of all kinds of things, our mother obviously hated to accept. What I later understood was that my mother was making a desperate effort to preserve her pride, and ours. Pride was just about all we had to preserve, for by 1934, we really began to suffer."

Contrary to a widespread assumption that has crept back into Anglo-American political jargon, few derive pleasure from handouts: of clothes, shoes, food, rent support or children's school supplies. It is, quite simply, humiliating. Restoring pride and self-respect to society's losers was a central platform in the social reforms that marked 20th century progress. Today we have once again turned our back on them.

Although uncritical admiration for the Anglo-Saxon model of "free enterprise", "the private sector", "efficiency", "profits" and "growth" has been widespread in recent years, the model itself has only been applied in all its self-congratulatory rigor in

Ireland, the UK and the USA. Of Ireland there is little to say. The so-called "economic miracle" of the 'plucky little Celtic tiger' consisted of an unregulated, low-tax regime which predictably attracted inward investment and hot money. The inevitable shortfall in public income was compensated by subsidies from the much-maligned European Union, funded for the most part by the supposedly inept 'old European' economies of Germany, France and the Netherlands. When Wall Street's party crashed, the Irish bubble burst along with it. It will not soon reflate.

The British case is more interesting: it mimics the very worst features of America while failing to open the UK to the social and educational mobility which characterized American progress at its best. On the whole, the British economy since 1979 tracked the decline of its American *confrère* not only in a cavalier unconcern for its victims but also in a reckless enthusiasm for financial services at the expense of the country's industrial base. Whereas bank assets as a share of GDP had remained steady at around 70% from the 1880s through the early 1970s, by 2005 they exceeded 500%. As aggregate national wealth grew, so did the poverty of most of the regions outside London and north of the river Trent.

To be sure, even Margaret Thatcher could not altogether dismantle the welfare state, popular with the same lower middle class that so enthusiastically brought her to power. And thus, in contrast to the United States, the growing number of people at the bottom of the British heap still have access to free or cheap medical services, exiguous but guaranteed pensions, residual unemployment relief and a vestigial system of public education. If Britain is "broken", as some observers have concluded in recent years, at least the constituent fragments get caught in a safety net. For a society trapped in delusions of prosperity and good prospects, with the losers left to fend for themselves, we must—regretfully—look to the USA.

AMERICAN PECULIARITIES

"As one digs deeper into the national character of the Americans, one sees that they have sought the value of everything in this world only in the answer to this single question: how much money will it bring in?"

—ALEXIS DE TOCQUEVILLE

Without knowing anything about OECD charts or unfavorable comparisons with other nations, many Americans are well aware that something is seriously amiss. They do not live as well as they once did. Everyone would like their child to have improved life chances at birth: better education and better job prospects. They would prefer it if their wife or daughter had the same odds of surviving maternity as women in other advanced countries. They would appreciate full medical coverage at lower cost, longer life expectancy, better public services, and less crime. However, when advised that such benefits are available in Western Europe, many Americans respond: "But they have socialism! We do not want the state interfering in our affairs. And above all, we do not wish to pay more taxes."

This curious cognitive dissonance is an old story. A century ago, the German sociologist Werner Sombart famously asked: *Why is there no socialism in America?* There are many answers to this question. Some have to do with the sheer size of the country: shared purposes are difficult to organize and sustain on an imperial scale and the US is, for all practical purposes, an inland empire.

Then there are cultural factors, notorious among them the distinctively American suspicion of central government. Whereas certain very large and diverse territorial units—China, for example, or Brazil—depend upon the powers and initiatives of a distant state, the US, in this respect unmistakably a child of 18th century Anglo-Scottish thought, was built on the premise that the power of central authority should be hemmed in on all sides. The presumption in the American Bill of Rights—that whatever is not explicitly accorded to the national government is by default the prerogative of the separate states—has been internalized over the course of the centuries by generations of settlers and immigrants as a license to keep Washington "out of our lives".

This suspicion of the public authorities, periodically elevated to a cult by Know Nothings, States' Rightists, anti-tax campaigners and—most recently—the radio talk show demagogues of the Republican Right, is uniquely American. It translates an already distinctive suspicion of taxation (with or without representation) into patriotic dogma. Here in the US, taxes are typically regarded as uncompensated income loss. The idea that they might (also) be a contribution to the provision of collective goods that individuals could never afford in isolation (roads, firemen, policemen, schools, lamp posts, post offices, not to mention soldiers, warships, and weapons) is rarely considered.

In continental Europe as in much of the developed world, the idea that any one person could be completely 'self-made' evaporated with the illusions of 19th century individualism. We are all the beneficiaries of those who went before us, as well as those who will care for us in old age or ill health. We all depend upon services whose costs we share with our fellow citizens, however selfishly we conduct our economic lives. But in America, the ideal of the autonomous entrepreneurial individual remains as appealing as ever.

And yet, the United States has not always been at odds with the rest of the modern world. Even if that were the case for the America of Andrew Jackson or Ronald Reagan, it hardly does justice to the far-reaching social reforms of the New Deal or Lyndon Johnson's Great Society in the 1960s. After visiting Washington in 1934, Maynard Keynes wrote to Felix Frankfurter: "Here, not in Moscow, is the economic laboratory of the world. The young men who are running it are splendid. I am astonished at their competence, intelligence and wisdom. One meets a classical economist here and there who ought to be thrown out of [the] window—but they mostly have been."

Much the same might have been said of the remarkable ambitions and achievements of the Democratic-led Congresses of the '60s that created food stamps, Medicare, the Civil Rights Act, Medicaid, Headstart, the National Endowment for the Humanities, the National Endowment for the Arts and the Corporation for Public Broadcasting. If this was America, it bore a curious resemblance to 'old Europe'.

Moreover, the 'public sector' in American life is in some respects more articulated, developed and respected than its European counterparts. The best instance of this is the public provision of first-class institutions of higher education—something that the US has done for longer and better than most European countries. The land grant colleges that became the University of California, the University of Indiana, the University of Michigan and other internationally renowned institutions have no peers outside the US, and the often underestimated community college system is similarly unique.

Moreover, for all their inability to sustain a national railway system, Americans not only networked their country with tax-payer-financed freeways; today, they support in some of their major cities well-functioning systems of public transport at the very moment that their English counterparts can think of nothing better to do than dump the latter on the private sector at fire-sale prices. To be sure, the citizens of the US remain unable to furnish themselves with even the minimal decencies of a public health system; but 'public' as such was not always a term of opprobrium in the national lexicon.

ECONOMISM AND ITS DISCONTENTS

"Once we allow ourselves to be disobedient to the test of an accountant's profit, we have begun to change our civilization."

—JOHN MAYNARD KEYNES

Why do we experience such difficulty even *imagining* a different sort of society? Why is it beyond us to conceive of a different set of arrangements to our common advantage? Are we doomed indefinitely to lurch between a dysfunctional 'free market' and the much-advertised horrors of 'socialism'?

Our disability is *discursive*: we simply do not know how to talk about these things any more. For the last thirty years, when asking ourselves whether we support a policy, a proposal or an initiative, we have restricted ourselves to issues of profit and loss—economic questions in the narrowest sense. But this is not an instinctive human condition: it is an acquired taste.

We have been here before. In 1905, the young William Beveridge—whose 1942 report would lay the foundations of the British welfare state—delivered a lecture at Oxford, asking why political philosophy had been obscured in public debates by classical economics. Beveridge's question applies with equal force today. However, this eclipse of political thought bears no relation to the writings of the great classical economists themselves.

Indeed, the thought that we might restrict public policy considerations to a mere economic calculus was already a source of concern two centuries ago. The Marquis de Condorcet, one of the most perceptive writers on commercial capitalism in its early years, anticipated with distaste the prospect that "liberty will be no more, in the eyes of an avid nation, than the necessary condition for the security of financial operations." The revolutions of the age risked fostering confusion between the freedom to make money . . . and freedom itself.

We too are confused. Conventional economic reasoning today—ostensibly bloodied but apparently quite unbowed by its inability either to foresee or prevent the banking collapse—describes human behavior in terms of 'rational choice'. We are all, it asserts, economic beings. We pursue our self-interest (defined as maximized economic advantage) with minimal reference to extraneous criteria such as altruism, self-denial, taste, cultural habit or collective purpose. Supplied with sufficient and correct information about 'markets'—whether real ones or institutions for the sale and purchase of stocks and bonds—we shall make the best possible choices to our separate and common advantage.

Whether or not these propositions hold any truth is not my concern here. No one today could claim with a straight face that anything remains of the so-called 'efficient market hypothesis'. An older generation of free market economists used to point out that what is wrong with socialist planning is that it requires the sort of perfect knowledge (of present and future alike) that is never vouchsafed to ordinary mortals. They were right. But it transpires that the same is true for market theorists: they don't know everything and as a result it turns out that they don't really know anything.

The 'false precision' of which Maynard Keynes accused his economist critics is with us still. Worse: we have smuggled in a misleadingly 'ethical' vocabulary to bolster our economic arguments, furnishing us with a self-satisfied gloss upon crassly utilitarian calculations. When imposing welfare cuts on the poor, for example, legislators in the UK and US alike have taken a singular pride in the 'hard choices' they have had to make.

The poor vote in much smaller numbers than anyone else. So there is little political risk in penalizing them: just how 'hard' are such choices? These days, we take pride in being tough enough to inflict pain on others. If an older usage were still in force, whereby being tough consisted of *enduring* pain rather than imposing it on others, we should perhaps think twice before so callously valuing efficiency over compassion.[4]

In that case, how *should* we talk about the way we choose to run our societies? In the first place, we cannot continue to evaluate our world and the choices we make in a moral vacuum. Even if we could be sure that a sufficiently well-informed and self-aware rational individual would always opt for his own best interests, we would still need to ask just what those interests *are*. They cannot be inferred from his economic behavior, for in that case the argument would be circular. We need to ask what men and women want for themselves and under what conditions those wants may be addressed.

Clearly we cannot do without *trust*. If we truly did not trust one another, we would not pay taxes for our mutual support. Nor would we venture very far outdoors for fear of violence or chicanery at the hands of our untrustworthy fellow citizens. Moreover, trust is no abstract virtue. One of the reasons that capitalism today is under siege from so many critics, by no means all of them on the Left, is that markets and free competition also require trust and cooperation. If we cannot trust

---

4 Avner Offer, *The Challenge of Affluence: Self-Control and Well-Being in the United States and Britain since 1950* (Oxford: Oxford University Press, 2007), p. 7.

bankers to behave honestly, or mortgage brokers to tell the truth about their loans, or public regulators to blow the whistle on dishonest traders, then capitalism itself will grind to a halt.

Markets do not automatically generate trust, cooperation or collective action for the common good. Quite the contrary: it is in the nature of economic competition that a participant who breaks the rules will triumph—at least in the short run—over more ethically sensitive competitors. But capitalism could not survive such cynical behavior for very long. So why has this potentially self-destructive system of economic arrangements lasted? Probably because of habits of restraint, honesty and moderation which accompanied its emergence.

However, far from inhering in the nature of capitalism itself, values such as these derived from longstanding religious or communitarian practices. Sustained by traditional restraints and the continuing authority of secular and ecclesiastical elites, capitalism's 'invisible hand' benefited from the flattering illusion that it unerringly corrected for the moral shortcomings of its practitioners.

These happy inaugural conditions no longer obtain. A contract-based market economy cannot generate them from within, which is why both socialist critics and religious commentators (notably the early 20th century reforming Pope Leo XIII) drew attention to the corrosive threat posed to society by unregulated economic markets and immoderate extremes of wealth and poverty.

As recently as the 1970s, the idea that the point of life was to get rich and that governments existed to facilitate this would have been ridiculed: not only by capitalism's traditional critics but also by many of its staunchest defenders. Relative indifference to wealth for its own sake was widespread in the postwar decades. In a survey of English schoolboys taken in 1949, it was discovered that the more intelligent the boy the more likely he was to choose an interesting career at a reasonable wage over a job that would merely pay well.[5] Today's schoolchildren and college students can imagine little else but the search for a lucrative job.

How should we begin to make amends for raising a generation obsessed with the pursuit of material wealth and indifferent to so much else? Perhaps we might start by reminding ourselves and our children that it wasn't always thus. Thinking 'economistically', as we have done now for thirty years, is not intrinsic to humans. There was a time when we ordered our lives differently.

5   T. H. Marshall, *Citizenship and Social Class* (London: Pluto Press, 1991), p. 48.

CHAPTER TWO

The World We Have Lost

> *"All of us know by now that from this
> war there is no way back to a laissez-
> faire order of society, that war as such is
> the maker of a silent revolution by
> preparing the road to a new type of
> planned order."*
>
> —KARL MANNHEIM, 1943

The past was neither as good nor as bad as we suppose: it was just different. If we tell ourselves nostalgic stories, we shall never engage the problems that face us in the present—and the same is true if we fondly suppose that our own world is better in every way. The past really is another country: we cannot go back. However, there is something worse than idealizing the past—or presenting it to ourselves and our children as a chamber of horrors: forgetting it.

Between the two world wars Americans, Europeans and much of the rest of the world faced a series of unprecedented man-made disasters. The First World War, already the worst and most intensely destructive in recorded memory, was followed in short order by epidemics, revolutions, the failure and breakup of states, currency collapses and unemployment on a scale never conceived by the traditional economists whose policies were still in vogue.

These developments in turn precipitated the fall of most of the world's democracies into autocratic dictatorships or totalitarian party states of various kinds and tipped the globe into a second World War even more destructive than the first. In Europe, in the Middle East, in east and southeast Asia, the years between 1931 and 1945 saw occupation, destruction, ethnic cleansing, torture, wars of extermination and deliberate genocide on a scale that would have been unimaginable even 30 years earlier.

As late as 1942, it seemed reasonable to fear for freedom. Outside of the English-speaking lands of the north Atlantic and Australasia, democracy was thin on the ground. The only democracies left in continental Europe were the tiny neutral states of Sweden and Switzerland, both dependent on German goodwill. The US had just joined the war. Everything that we take for granted today was not only in jeopardy, but seriously questioned even by its defenders.

Surely, it seemed, the future lay with the dictatorships? Even after the Allies emerged triumphant in 1945, these concerns were not forgotten: depression and fascism remained ever-present in men's minds. The urgent question was not how to celebrate a magnificent victory and get back to business as usual, but how on earth to ensure that the experience of the years 1914-1945 would never be repeated. More than anyone else, it was Maynard Keynes who devoted himself to addressing this challenge.

The Keynesian Consensus

*"In those years each one of us derived strength
from the common upswing of the time and
increased his individual confidence out of the
collective confidence. Perhaps, thankless as we
human beings are, we did not realize then how
firmly and surely the wave bore us. But whoever
experienced that epoch of world confidence
knows that all since has been retrogression and
gloom."*

—Stefan Zweig

The great English economist (born in 1883) grew up in a stable, prosperous and powerful Britain: a confident world whose collapse he was privileged to observe—first from an influential perch at the wartime Treasury and then as a participant in the Versailles peace negotiations of 1919. The world of yesterday unraveled, taking with it not just countries, lives and material wealth but all the reassuring certainties of Keynes's culture and class. How had this happened? Why had no one foreseen it? Why was no one in authority doing anything effective to ensure that it would not happen again?

Understandably, Keynes focused his economic writings

upon the problem of *uncertainty*: in contrast to the confident nostrums of classical and neoclassical economics, he would insist henceforth upon the essential unpredictability of human affairs. To be sure, there were many lessons to be drawn from economic depression, fascist repression and wars of extermination. But more than anything else, as it seemed to Keynes, it was the new-found insecurity in which men and women were forced to live—uncertainty elevated to paroxysms of collective fear—which had corroded the confidence and institutions of liberalism.

What, then, should be done? Like so many others, Keynes was familiar with the attractions of centralized authority and top-down planning to compensate for the inadequacies of the market. Fascism and Communism shared an unabashed enthusiasm for deploying the state. Far from being a shortcoming in the popular eye, this was perhaps their strongest suit: when asked what they thought of Hitler long after his fall, foreigners would sometimes respond that he did at least put the Germans back to work. Whatever his failings, Stalin—it was often said—kept the Soviet Union clear of the Great Depression. And even the joke about Mussolini making Italian trains run on time had a certain edge: what's wrong with that?

Any attempt to put democracies back on their feet—or to bring democracy and political freedom to countries which had never had them—would have to engage with the record of the authoritarian states. The alternative was to risk popular nostalgia for their achievements—real or imagined. Keynes knew perfectly well that fascist economic policy could never have succeeded in the long-run without war, occupation and exploitation. Nonetheless, he was sensitive not just to the need for countercyclical economic policies to head off future depression, but also to the prudential virtues of 'the social security state'.

The point of such a state was not to revolutionize social relations, much less inaugurate a socialist era. Keynes, like most of the men responsible for the innovative legislation of those years—from Britain's Clement Attlee through France's Charles de Gaulle to Franklin Delano Roosevelt himself—was an instinctive conservative. Every western leader in those years—elderly gentlemen all—had been born into the stable world so familiar to Keynes. And all of them had lived through a traumatic upheaval. Like the hero of Giuseppe di Lampedusa's *Leopard*, they understood very well that in order to conserve you must change.

Keynes died in 1946, exhausted by his wartime labors. But he had long since demonstrated that neither capitalism nor liberalism would survive very long without one another. And since the experience of the interwar years had clearly revealed the inability of capitalists to protect their own best interests, the liberal state would have to do it for them whether they liked it or not.

It is thus an intriguing paradox that capitalism was to be saved—indeed, was to thrive in the coming decades—thanks to changes identified at the time (and since) with socialism. This, in turn, reminds us just how very desperate circumstances were. Intelligent conservatives—like the many Christian Democrats who found themselves in office after 1945 for the first time—offered little objection to state control of the "commanding heights" of the economy; along with steeply progressive taxation, they welcomed it enthusiastically.

There was a *moralized* quality to policy debates in those early postwar years. Unemployment (the biggest issue in the UK, the US or Belgium); inflation (the greatest fear in central Europe, where it had ravaged private savings for decades); and agricultural prices so low (in Italy and France) that peasants were driven off the land and into extremist parties out of despair: these were not just economic issues, they were regarded by everyone from priests to secular intellectuals as tests of the ethical coherence of the community.

The consensus was unusually broad. From the New Dealers to West German "social market" theorists, from Britain's governing Labour Party to the "indicative" economic planning that shaped public policy in France (and Czechoslovakia, until the 1948 Communist coup): everyone believed in the state. In part, this was because almost everyone feared the implications of a return to the terrors of the recent past and was happy to constrain the freedom of the market in the name of the public interest. Just as the world was now to be regulated and protected by a bevy of international institutions and agreements, from the United Nations to the World Bank, so a well-run democracy would likewise maintain consensus around comparable domestic arrangements.

As early as 1940, Evan Durbin (a British Labour pamphleteer) had written that he could not imagine "the least alteration" in the contemporary trend towards collective bargaining, economic planning, progressive taxation and the provision of publicly funded social services. Sixteen years later, the English Labour politician Anthony Crosland could write, with still greater confidence, that there had been a permanent transition from "an uncompromising faith in individualism and self-help to a belief in group action and participation". He could even assert that "[a]s for the dogma of the 'invisible hand' and the belief that private gain must always lead to the public good, these failed entirely to survive the Great Depression; and even Conservatives and businessmen now subscribe to the doctrine of collective government responsible for the state of the economy".[6]

Durbin and Crosland were both social democrats and thus interested parties. But they were not wrong. By the mid-'50s English politics had reached such a level of implied consensus around public policy issues that mainstream political argument was dubbed "Butskellism": blending the ideas of R.A. Butler, a moderate Conservative minister and Hugh Gaitskell, the centrist leader of the Labour opposition in those years. And Butskellism was universal. Whatever their other differences, French Gaullists, Christian Democrats and Socialists shared a common faith in the activist state, economic planning and large-scale public investment. Much the same was true of the consensus that dominated policy-making in Scandinavia, the Benelux countries, Austria and even ideologically-riven Italy.

In Germany, where social democrats persisted in their Marxist rhetoric (if not Marxist policies) until 1959, there was nevertheless comparatively little separating them from Chancellor Konrad Adenauer's Christian Democrats. Indeed, it was the (to them) stifling consensus on everything from education to foreign policy to the public provision of recreational

6 Anthony Crosland, *The Future of Socialism* (London: Jonathan Cape, 1956), pp. 105, 65.

facilities—and the interpretation of their country's troubled past—that drove a younger generation of German radicals into "extra-parliamentary" activity.

Even in the United States, where Republicans were in power throughout the '50s and aging New Dealers found themselves in the wilderness for the first time in a generation, the transition to conservative administrations—while it had significant consequences for foreign affairs and even free speech—made little difference to domestic policy. Taxation was not a contentious issue and it was a Republican president, Dwight Eisenhower, who authorized the massive, federally-overseen project of the interstate highway system. For all the lip service paid to competition and free markets, the American economy in those years depended heavily upon protection from foreign competition, as well as standardization, regulation, subsidies, price supports, and government guarantees.

The natural inequities of capitalism were softened by the assurance of present well-being and future prosperity. In the mid-'60s, Lyndon Johnson pushed through a series of path-breaking social and cultural changes; he was able to do so in part because of the residual consensus favoring New Deal-style investments, all-inclusive programs and government initiatives. Significantly, it was civil rights and race relation legislation that divided the country, not social policy.

The years 1945—1975 were widely acknowledged as something of a miracle, giving birth to the 'American way of life'. Two generations of Americans—the men and women who went through WWII and their children who were to celebrate the '60s—experienced job security and upward social mobility on an unprecedented (and never to be repeated) scale. In Germany, the *Wirtschaftswunder* (economic miracle) lifted the country in a single generation from humiliating, rubble-strewn defeat into the wealthiest state in Europe. For France, those years were to become famous (with no hint of irony) as "Les Trente Glorieuses". In England, at the height of the "age of affluence", the Conservative Prime Minister Harold Macmillan assured his compatriots that "you have never had it so good". He was right.

In some countries (Scandinavia being the best-known case) the postwar welfare states were the work of social democrats; elsewhere—in Great Britain, for example—the "social security state" amounted in practice to little more than a series of pragmatic policies aimed at alleviating disadvantage and reducing extremes of wealth and indigence. Their common accomplishment was a remarkable success in curbing inequality. If we compare the gap separating rich and poor, whether measured by overall assets or annual income, we find that in every continental European country as well as in Great Britain and the US, the gap shrank dramatically in the generation following 1945.

With greater equality there came other benefits. Over time, the fear of a return to extremist politics abated. The 'West' entered a halcyon era of prosperous security: a bubble, perhaps, but a comforting bubble in which most people did far better than they could ever have hoped in the past and had good reason to anticipate the future with confidence.

Moreover, it was social democracy and the welfare state that bound the professional and commercial middle classes to liberal institutions in the wake of World War II. This was a matter of some consequence: it was the fear and disaffection of the middle class which had given rise to fascism. Bonding the middle classes back to the democracies was by far the most important task facing postwar politicians—and by no means an easy one.

In most cases it was achieved by the magic of "universalism". Instead of having their benefits keyed to income—in which case well-paid professionals or thriving shopkeepers might have complained bitterly at being taxed for social services from which *they* did not derive much advantage—the educated "middling sort" were offered the same social assistance and public services as the working population and the poor: free education, cheap or free medical treatment, public pensions and unemployment insurance. As a consequence, now that so many of life's necessities were covered by their taxes, the

European middle class found itself by the 1960s with far greater disposable incomes than at any time since 1914.

Interestingly, these decades were characterized by a uniquely successful blend of social innovation and cultural conservatism. Keynes himself exemplifies the point. A man of impeccably elitist tastes and upbringing—though unusually open to new artistic work—he nonetheless grasped the importance of bringing first-class art, performance and writing to the broadest possible audience if British society were to overcome its paralyzing divisions. It was Keynes whose initiatives led to the creation of the Royal Ballet, the Arts Council and much else besides. These were innovative public provisions of uncompromisingly "high" art—much like Lord Reith's BBC, with its self-assigned obligation to raise popular standards rather than condescend to them.

For Reith or Keynes or the French Culture Minister André Malraux, there was nothing patronizing about this new approach—any more than there was for the young Americans who worked with LBJ on the establishment of a Corporation for Public Broadcasting or the National Endowment for the Humanities. This was "meritocracy": the opening up of elite institutions to mass applicants at public expense—or at least underwritten by public assistance. It began the process of replacing selection by inheritance or wealth with upward mobility through education. And it produced a few years later a generation for whom all of this seemed self-evident and who thus took it for granted.

There was nothing inevitable about these developments. Wars were typically followed by economic downturns—and the bigger the war the worse the dip. Those who did not fear a resurgence of fascism looked instead anxiously eastwards at the hundreds of divisions of the Red Army and the powerful, popular Communist parties and trade unions of Italy, France and Belgium. When US Secretary of State George Marshall visited Europe in the spring of 1947 he was appalled by what he saw: the Marshall Plan was born of the anxiety that the aftermath of World War II might end up even worse than that of its predecessor.

As for the US, it was deeply divided in those early postwar years by a renascent suspicion of foreigners, radicals and above all communists. McCarthyism may have posed no threat to the Republic, but it was a reminder of just how easily a mediocre demagogue could exploit fear and exaggerate threats. What might he not have done had the economy reverted to its low point of twenty years before? In short, and despite the consensus that was to emerge, it was all more than a little unexpected. So why did it work so well?

THE REGULATED MARKET

"The idea is essentially repulsive, of a society held together only by the relations and feelings arising out of pecuniary interest."

—JOHN STUART MILL

The short answer is that by 1945 few people believed any longer in the magic of the market. This was an intellectual revolution. Classical economics mandated a tiny role for the state in economic policymaking, and the prevailing liberal ethos of 19th century Europe and North America favored hands-off social legislation, confined for the most part to regulating only the more egregious inequities and dangers of competitive industrialism and financial speculation.

But two world wars had habituated almost everyone to the inevitability of government intervention in daily life. In the First World War most of the participant states had increased their control (hitherto negligible) of production: not just of military *matériel* but clothing, transport, communications and almost anything relevant to the conduct of an expensive and desperate war. In most places after 1918 these controls were lifted, but there remained a significant residue of government involvement in the regulation of economic life.

Following a short, illusory era of retreat (marked symptomatically by the ascendancy of Calvin Coolidge in the United States and by comparably negligent types in much of western Europe), the utter devastation of the 1929 slump and the ensuing depression forced all governments to choose between ineffectual reticence and overt intervention. Sooner or later, all would opt for the latter.

Whatever remained of the laissez-faire state was then erased by the experience of total war. With no exception, winners and losers in World War II committed not just the country, the economy and every citizen to the pursuit of war; they also mobilized the state for this purpose in ways which would have been inconceivable just thirty years earlier. Whatever their political colour, the combatant states mobilized, regulated, directed, planned and administered every aspect of life.

Even in the United States, the job you held, the wage you were paid, the things you could buy and the places you might go were all constrained in ways that would have horrified Americans a few short years before. The New Deal, whose agencies and institutions had seemed so shockingly innovatory, could now be seen as a mere prelude to the business of mobilizing the whole country around a collective project.

War, in short, concentrated the mind. It had proven possible to convert a whole country into a war machine around a war economy; why then, people asked, could something similar not be accomplished in pursuit of peace? There was no convincing answer. Without anyone quite intending it, western Europe and North America entered upon a new era.

The most obvious symptom of the change came in the form of 'planning'. Rather than letting things just happen, economists and bureaucrats concluded, it was better to think them out in advance. Unsurprisingly, planning was most admired and advocated at the political extremes. On the Left it was thought that planning was what the Soviets did so well; on the Right it was (correctly) believed that Hitler, Mussolini and their fascist acolytes were committed to top-down planning and that this accounted for their appeal.

The intellectual case for planning was never very strong. Keynes, as we have seen, regarded economic planning much as he did pure market theory: in order to succeed, both required impossibly perfect data. But he accepted, at least in wartime, the necessity of short-term planning and controls. For the postwar peace, he preferred to minimize direct government intervention and manipulate the economy through fiscal and other incentives. But for this to work, governments needed to know what they wished to achieve and this, in the eyes of its advocates, was what 'planning' was all about.

Curiously, the enthusiasm for planning was especially

marked in the United States. The Tennessee Valley Authority was nothing if not an exercise in confident economic design: not just of a vital resource but of the economy of a whole region. Observers like Louis Mumford declared themselves "entitled to a little collective strutting and crowing": the TVA and similar projects showed that democracies could match the dictatorships when it came to large-scale, long-term, forward-looking schemes. A few years earlier, Rexford Tugwell had gone so far as to eulogize the idea: "I see the great plan already/And the keen joy of the work will be mine . . . /I shall roll up my sleeves—make/America over."[7]

The difference between a planned economy and a state-owned economy was still unclear to many. Liberals like Keynes, William Beveridge or Jean Monnet, the founding spirit behind French planning, had no time for nationalization as an objective in its own right, though they were flexible as to its practical advantages in particular cases. The same was true of the Social Democrats of Scandinavia: far more interested in progressive taxation and the provision of all-embracing social services than in state control of major industries—car manufacturing, for example.

---

7 Robert Leighninger, *Long-Range Public Investment: The Forgotten Legacy of the New Deal* (Columbia, SC: University of South Carolina Press, 2007), pp. 117, 169.

Conversely, Britain's Labourites doted on the idea of public ownership. If the state represented the working population, then surely a state-owned operation was henceforth in the hands and at the disposal of the workers? Whether or not this was true in practice—the history of British Steel suggests that the state can be just as incompetent and inefficient as the worst private entrepreneur—it diverted attention from any sort of planning at all, with detrimental consequences in decades to come. At the other extreme, Communist planning—which amounted to little more than the establishment of fictional targets to be met by fictional output data—would in due course discredit the whole exercise.

In continental Europe, centralized administrations had traditionally played a more active role in the provision of social services and continued to do so on a greatly expanded scale. The market, it was widely held, was inadequate to the task of defining collective ends: the state would have to step in and fill the breach. Even in the USA, where the state—the "Administration"—was always wary of overstepping traditional bounds, everything from the GI Bill to the scientific education of the coming generation was initiated and paid for from Washington.

Here, too, it was simply assumed that there were public goods and goals for which the market was just not suited. In the words of T.H. Marshall, a leading commentator on the British welfare state, the whole point of 'welfare' is to "supersede the market by taking goods and services out of it, or in some way to control and modify its operations so as to produce a result it could not have produced itself."[8]

Even in West Germany, where there was an understandable reluctance to pursue Nazi-style centralized controls, 'social market theorists' compromised. They insisted that the free market was compatible with social goals and welfare legislation: it would actually function best if encouraged to perform with these objectives in mind. Hence the legislation, much of it still in force, requiring banks and public companies to take the long view, listen to the interests of their employees and maintain an awareness of the social consequences of their business even while pursuing profits.

That the state might exceed its remit and damage the market by distorting its operations was not taken very seriously in these years. From the institution of an International Monetary Fund and a World Bank (later a World Trade Organization as well) to international clearing houses, currency controls, wage restrictions and indicative price limits, the emphasis lay rather

8 Neil Gilbert, *The Transformation of the Welfare State: The Silent Surrender of Public Responsibility* (New York: Oxford University Press, 2004), p. 135.

in the need to compensate for the palpable shortcomings of markets.

For the same reason, high taxation was not regarded in these years as an affront. On the contrary, steep rates of progressive income tax were seen as a consensual device to take excess resources away from the privileged and the useless and place them at the disposal of those who needed them most or could use them best. This too was not a new idea. The income tax had started to bite in most European countries well before the First World War, and had continued to increase between the wars in many places. All the same, as recently as 1925, most middle class families could still afford one, two or even more servants—often in residence.

By 1950, however, only the aristocracy and the *nouveaux riches* could hope to maintain such a household: between taxes, inheritance duties and a steady increase in jobs and wages available to the working population, the labor pool of impoverished and subservient domestic employees had all but dried up. Thanks to universal welfare provision, the one benefit of long-term domestic service—the presumptive generosity of the employer for his sick, aged or otherwise indisposed servant—was now redundant.

In the general population there was a widespread belief that a moderate redistribution of wealth, eliminating extremes of rich and poor, was to everyone's benefit. Condorcet had wisely observed that, "[i]t will always be cheaper for the Treasury to put the poor in a position to buy corn, than to bring the price of corn down to within the reach of the poor."[9] By 1960 this thesis had become de facto government policy throughout the West.

A generation or two later, these attitudes must seem curious indeed. For three decades following the war, economists, politicians, commentators and citizens all agreed that high public expenditure, administered by local or national authorities with considerable latitude to regulate economic life at many levels, was good policy. Dissenters were regarded as either curiosities from a forgotten past—mad ideologues pursuing unworldly theorems—or else self-interested advocates of private advantage over public well-being. The market was kept in its place, the state accorded a central role in peoples' lives and social services given precedent over other government expenditure—except, partially, in the American case where military outlays continued to grow apace.

How could this have been? Even if we were willing to concede that such collectivist goals and practices were admirable in principle, we should today regard them as inefficient—because

---

9 Marquis de Condorcet, *Reflexions sur le commerce des bles* (1776) in *Oeuvres de Condorcet* (Paris: Firmin Didot, 1847-1849), p. 231. Quoted in Emma Rothschild, *Economic Sentiments: Adam Smith, Condorcet and the Enlightenment* (Cambridge: Harvard University Press, 2002), p. 78.

of their diversion of private funds into public purposes—and in any case dangerously likely to hand economic and social resources to "bureaucrats", "politicians" and "big government". Why were our parents and our grandparents so little troubled by such considerations? Why did they so readily concede initiative to the public sector and hand over private wealth in pursuit of collective goals?

COMMUNITY, TRUST AND COMMON PURPOSE

> *"To feel much for others and little for ourselves; to restrain our selfishness and exercise our benevolent affections, constitute the perfection of human nature."*
>
> —ADAM SMITH

All collective undertakings require trust. From the games that children play to complex social institutions, humans cannot work together unless they suspend their suspicion of one another. One person holds the rope, another jumps. One person steadies the ladder, another climbs. Why? In part because we hope for reciprocity, but in part from what is clearly a natural propensity to work in cooperation to collective advantage.

Taxation is a revealing illustration of this truth. When we

pay taxes, we make quite a lot of assumptions about our fellow citizens. In the first instance, we assume that they will pay their taxes too, or else we would feel unfairly burdened and would in due course withhold our own contributions. Secondly, we trust those we have placed in temporary authority over us to collect and spend the cash responsibly. After all, by the time we discover that they have embezzled or wasted it, we shall have lost a lot of money.

Thirdly, most taxation goes towards either paying off past debt or investing in future expenditures. Accordingly, there is an implicit relationship of trust and mutuality between past taxpayers and present beneficiaries, present taxpayers and past and future recipients—and of course future taxpayers who will cover the cost of our outlays today. We are thus condemned to trust not only people we don't know today, but people we could never have known and people we shall never know, with all of whom we have a complicated relationship of mutual interest.

The same point applies to public expenditure. If we raise taxes or put up a bond to pay for a school in our home district, the chances are that other people (and other peoples' children) will be the chief beneficiaries. The same applies to public investment in light rail systems, long-term educational and research projects, medical science, social security contributions and any other collective expenditure whose pay-off may lie years away. So why do we go to the trouble of putting up the money? Because others have put up money in the past for us and, usually without giving the matter too much thought, we see ourselves as part of a civic community transcending generations.

But who is 'we'? Whom exactly do we trust? The English conservative philosopher Michael Oakeshott regarded politics as dependent on a definition of the community of trust: "Politics is the activity of attending to the general arrangements of a collection of people who, in respect of their common recognition of a manner of attending to its arrangements, compose a single community."[10] But this definition is circular: which particular collection of people recognizes a common way of 'attending to its arrangements'? The whole world? Clearly not. Would we expect a resident of Omaha, Nebraska to enjoy paying taxes for the provision of bridges and highways in Kuala Lumpur on the implied understanding that his Malaysian equivalent will be voluntarily doing likewise for him? No.

So what is it that defines the workable scope of a community of trust? Rootless cosmopolitanism is fine for intellectuals, but most people live in a defined place: defined by space, by

10 Michael Oakeshott, *Rationalism in Politics and Other Essays* (New York: Basic Books, 1962), p. 56.

time, by language, perhaps by religion, maybe—however regrettably—by color, and so forth. Such places are fungible. Most Europeans would not have defined themselves as living in 'Europe' until very recently: they would have said they lived in Lodz (Poland), or Liguria (Italy) or perhaps even 'Putney' (a suburb of London).

The sense of being 'European' for purposes of self-identification is a newly acquired habit. As a result, where the idea of transnational cooperation or mutual assistance might have aroused intense local suspicion, today it passes largely unnoticed. Dutch dockworkers today subsidize Portuguese fishermen and Polish farmers without too much complaint; in part, no doubt, this is because the dockworkers in question don't interrogate too closely their political masters as to the use being made of their taxes. But this too is a sign of trust.

There is quite a lot of evidence that people trust other people more if they have a lot in common with them: not just religion or language but also income. The more equal a society, the greater the trust. And it is not just a question of income: where people have similar lives and similar prospects, it is likely that what we might call their 'moral outlook' is also shared. This makes it much easier to institute radical departures in public policy. In complex or divided societies, the chances are that a minority—or even a majority—will be forced to concede,

often against its will. This makes collective policymaking contentious and favors a minimalist approach to social reform: better to do nothing than to divide people for and against a
controversial project.

The absence of trust is clearly inimical to a well-run society.
The great Jane Jacobs noted as much with respect to the very
practical business of urban life and the maintenance of cleanli-
ness and civility on city streets. If we don't trust each other, our
towns will look horrible and be nasty places to live. Moreover,
she observed, you cannot institutionalize trust. Once corroded, it
is virtually impossible to restore. And it needs care and nurturing
by the community—the collectivity—since with the best of in-
tentions no one person can make others trust him and be trusted
in return.

The kind of society where trust is widespread is likely to
be fairly compact and quite homogenous. The most developed
and successful welfare states of Europe are Finland, Sweden,
Norway, Denmark, the Netherlands and Austria, with Germany (formerly West Germany) as an interesting outlier. Most
of these countries have very small populations: of the Scandinavian lands only Sweden tops 6 million inhabitants and between them all they comprise less people than Tokyo. Even
Austria, at 8.2 million or the Netherlands, at 16.7 million are
tiny by world standards—Mumbai alone has more people than

Holland, and the whole population of Austria could be fitted into Mexico City . . . twice.

But it is not just a question of size. Like New Zealand, another small country (population 4.2 million, even smaller than Norway) that has succeeded in maintaining a high level of civic trust, the successful welfare states of northern Europe were remarkably homogenous. Until fairly recently it would only have been a slight exaggeration to say that most Norwegians, if they were not themselves farmers or fishermen, were their children. 94% of the population are of Norwegian stock, and 86% of them belong to the Church of Norway. In Austria, 92% of the population are self-ascribed 'Austrian' by origin (the figure was nearer 100% until the influx of Yugoslav refugees during the 1990s) and 83% of those who declared a religion in 2001 were Catholic.

Much the same is true of Finland, where 96% of those who declare a religion are officially Lutheran (and nearly all are Finns, saving only a small Swedish minority); Denmark, where 95% of the population affirm a Lutheran faith; and even the Netherlands—neatly divided between a primarily protestant north and the Catholic south, but where almost everyone who is not a member of the tiny, post-colonial minority of Indonesians, Turks, Surinamese and Moroccans defines themselves as 'Dutch'.

Contrast the United States: there will soon be no single majority ethnic group and a slight protestant majority among those affirming a religion is countered by a substantial Catholic minority (25%), not to mention significant Jewish and Muslim communities. The crossover case might be Canada: a mid-sized country (33 million people) with no dominant religion and a mere 66% of the population declaring themselves of European origin, but where trust and its accompanying social institutions seem to have taken root.

Size and homogeneity are of course not transferable. There is no way for India or the USA to become Austria or Norway, and in their purest form the social democratic welfare states of Europe are simply non-exportable: they have much the same appeal as a Volvo—and some similar limitations—and may be hard to sell to countries and cultures where expensive virtues of solidity and endurance count for less. We know, moreover, that even cities do better if they are reasonably homogenous and contained: it was not difficult to build municipal socialism in Vienna or Amsterdam, but would be a lot harder in Naples or Cairo, not to speak of Calcutta or Sao Paulo.

Finally, there is clear evidence that while homogeneity and size matter for the generation of trust and cooperation, cultural or economic heterogeneity can have the opposite effect. A steady increase in the number of immigrants, particularly immigrants from the 'third world', correlates all too well in the Netherlands and Denmark, not to mention the United Kingdom, with a noticeable decline in social cohesion. To put it bluntly, the Dutch and the English don't much care to share their welfare states with their former colonial subjects from Indonesia, Surinam, Pakistan or Uganda; meanwhile Danes, like Austrians, resent 'paying for' the Muslim refugees who have flocked to their countries in recent years.

There may be something inherently selfish in the social service states of the mid-20th century: blessed for a few decades with the good fortune of ethnic homogeneity and a small, educated population where almost everyone could recognize themselves in everyone else. Most of these countries—self-contained nation-states exposed to very little external threat—had the good fortune to cluster under the umbrella of NATO in the post-1945 decades, devoting their budgets to domestic improvement and untroubled by mass immigration from the rest of Europe, much less further afield. When this situation changed, confidence and trust appears to have fallen off.

However, the fact remains that trust and cooperation were crucial building blocks for the modern state, and the more trust there was the more successful the state. William Beveridge could assume in the England of his day a high measure of moral accord and civic engagement. Like so many liberals born in the late

19th century, he simply took it for granted that social cohesion was not merely a desirable goal but something of a given. Solidarity—with one's fellow citizens and with the state itself—pre-existed the welfare institutions which gave it public form.

Even in the United States the concept of trust and the desirability of fellow feeling became central to public policy debate from the 1930s forwards. It is arguable that the remarkable achievement of the US in converting itself from a semi-comatose peacetime economy into the world's greatest war machine would not have been possible without Roosevelt's insistence upon the shared interests and purposes and needs of *all* Americans. If World War II was a 'good war', it was not just thanks to the unambiguously awful character of our enemies. It was also because Americans felt good about America—and their fellow Americans.

Great Societies

"Our nation stands for democracy and proper drains."

—John Betjeman

What did trust, cooperation, progressive taxation and the interventionist state bequeath to western societies in the decades following 1945? The short answer is, in varying degrees, security, prosperity, social services and greater equality. We have grown accustomed in recent years to the assertion that the price paid for these benefits—in economic inefficiency, insufficient innovation, stifled entrepreneurship, public debt and a loss of private initiative—was too high.

Most of these criticisms are demonstrably false. Measured by the quality and quantity of the social legislation passed in the US between 1932 and 1971, America was unquestionably one of those 'good societies'; but few would wish to claim that the USA lacked initiative or entrepreneurship in those high, halcyon years of the American Century. But even if it were true that the European social democratic and social service states of the mid-20th century were economically unsustainable, this would not in itself vitiate their claims upon our attention.

Social democracy was always a mongrel politics. In the first place, it blended socialist dreams of a post-capitalist utopia with practical recognition of the need to live and work in a capitalist world that was demonstrably *not* on its last legs, as Marx had enthusiastically projected back in 1848. But secondly, social democracy took seriously the 'democracy' part: in contrast to the revolutionary socialists of the early 20th century and their communist successors, social democrats in free countries accepted the rules of the democratic game and compromised from early on with their critics and opponents as the price of competing for power.

Moreover, social democrats were not uniquely or even primarily interested in economics (in contrast to communists, who always emphasized economics as the measure of Marxist orthodoxy). Socialism for social democrats, especially in Scandinavia, was a *distributive* concept. It was about making sure that wealth and assets were not disproportionately gathered into the hands of a privileged few. And this, as we have seen, was in essence a moral matter: social democrats, like the 18th century critics of 'commercial society', were offended at the consequences of unregulated competition. They were seeking not so much a radical future as a return to the values of a better way of life.

Thus we should not be surprised to learn that an early English social democrat like Beatrice Webb took it for granted that the 'socialism' she sought could be parsed as public education, the public provision of health services and medical insurance, public parks and playgrounds, collective provision for the aged, infirm and unemployed and so on. The unity of the premodern world, its 'moral economy' as E.P. Thompson called it, was thus very much on her mind: people should cooperate, they should work together for the common good and no one should be left out.

Welfare states were not necessarily socialist in origin or purpose. They were the product of another sea change in public affairs that overtook the West between the '30s and the '60s: one that drew experts and scholars, intellectuals and technocrats into the business of administration. The result, at its best, was the American Social Security system, or Britain's National Health Service. Both were extraordinarily expensive innovations, breaking with the piecemeal reforms and repairs of the past.

The importance of such welfare undertakings did not lie in the ideas themselves—the thought that it would be good to guarantee all Americans a secure old age, or to make available to every British citizen first-class medical treatment at no point-of-service cost, was hardly original. But the thought that such things were best done by the government and that therefore they *should* be done by the government: this was unprecedented.

Precisely how such services and resources should be made available was always a contentious issue. Universalists, influential in Britain, favored high across-the-board taxation to pay for services and resources to which all would have equal access. Selectivists preferred to calibrate costs and benefits according to the needs and capacities of each citizen. These were practical choices, but they also reflected deeply held social and moral theories.

The Scandinavian model followed a more selective but also more ambitious program: its goal, as articulated by the influential Swedish sociologist Gunnar Myrdal, was to institutionalize the state's responsibility to "protect people against themselves."[11] Neither Americans nor British had any such ambitions. The idea that it was the state's business to know what was good for people—while we accept it uncomplainingly in school curriculums and hospital practices—smacked of eugenics and perhaps euthanasia.

Even at their height, the Scandinavian welfare states left the economy to the private sector—which was then taxed at very high rates to pay for social, cultural and other services. What Swedes, Finns, Danes and Norwegians offered themselves was

---

11 Quoted in Sheri Berman, *The Primacy of Politics: Social Democracy and the Making of Europe's Twentieth Century* (New York: Cambridge University Press, 2006), p. 207.

not collective ownership but the guarantee of collective *protection*. With the exception of Finland, Scandinavians all had private pension schemes—something that would have seemed very odd to the English or even most Americans in those days. But they looked to the state for almost everything else, and freely accepted the heavy hand of moral intrusion that this entailed.

The welfare states of continental Europe—what the French call the *Etat providence*, or providential state—followed yet a third model. Here, the emphasis was primarily on protecting the employed citizen against the ravages of the market economy. It should be noted that 'employed' here is no casual adjective. In France, Italy and West Germany it was the maintenance of jobs and incomes in the face of economic misfortune that preoccupied the welfare state.

To the American or even the modern English eye, this must seem peculiar indeed. Why protect a man or woman against the loss of a job which no longer produces anything people want? Surely it is better to acknowledge capitalism's 'creative destruction' and wait for better jobs to come along? But from the continental European perspective, the political implications of throwing large numbers of people onto the street at times of economic downturn were far more consequential than the hypothetical efficiency loss in maintaining 'unnecessary' jobs.

Like the 18th century guilds, French or German labor unions learned how to protect 'insiders'—men and women who already have secure employment—against 'outsiders': the young, the unskilled and others in search of work.

The effect of this sort of social protection state was and is to keep insecurity at bay—at the price of distorting the supposedly neutral workings of the labor market. The remarkable stability of continental societies which had experienced bloody turbulence and civil war only a few years before casts a favorable light upon the European model. Moreover, whereas the British and American economies have been ravaged by the financial crisis of 2008, with well over 16% of the American work force officially unemployed or no longer seeking work at the time of writing (February 2010), Germany and France have weathered the storm with a far lower level of human suffering and economic exclusion.

By protecting 'good' jobs at the price of failing to create more low-paying ones, France, Germany and other continental welfare states have made a deliberate choice. In the US and the UK, beginning in the 1970s, low-wage and insecure jobs began to replace the more stable employment of the boom years. Today, a young person might consider himself fortunate to find employment, at minimum wage and with no benefits, in Pizza Hut, Tesco or Walmart. Such openings are less easily come by in France or Germany. But who is to say, and on precisely what grounds, that someone is better off working for low wages at Walmart than she is taking unemployment pay on the European model? Most people would rather have work, to be sure. But at any price?

The priorities of the traditional state were defense, public order, the prevention of epidemics and the aversion of mass discontent. But following World War II, and peaking around 1980, social expenditure became the main budgetary responsibility for modern states. By 1988, with the notable exception of the United States, all the major developed countries were devoting more resources to welfare, broadly conceived, than to anything else. Understandably enough, taxes also rose sharply in these years.

For anyone old enough to remember what had gone before, this crescendo of social expenditure and welfare provision must have seemed little short of miraculous. The late Ralf Dahrendorf, an Anglo-German political scientist well placed to appreciate the scale of the changes he had seen in his lifetime, wrote of those optimistic years that "[i]n many respects the social democratic consensus signifies the greatest progress which history has seen so far. Never before have so many people had so many life chances."[12]

---

12 Ralf Dahrendorf, "The End of the Social Democratic Consensus" in *Life Chances* (Chicago: University of Chicago Press, 1979), pp. 108–9.

He was not mistaken. Not only did social democrats and welfare governments sustain full employment for nearly three decades, they also maintained growth rates more than competitive with those of the untrammeled market economies of the past. And on the back of these economic successes they introduced radically disjunctive social changes that came to seem, within a short span of years, quite normal. When Lyndon Johnson spoke of building a 'great society' on the basis of massive public expenditure on a variety of government-supported programs and agencies, few objected and fewer still thought the proposition odd.

By the early '70s it would have appeared unthinkable to contemplate unraveling the social services, welfare provisions, state-funded cultural and educational resources and much else that people had come to take for granted. To be sure, there were those who pointed to a likely imbalance between public income and expenditure as the pension bills grew and the baby boom generation aged. The institutional costs of legislating social justice in so many spheres of human activity were inevitably considerable: access to higher education, public provision of legal aid to the indigent and cultural subsidies for the arts did not come free. Moreover, as the postwar boom wound down and endemic unemployment once again became a serious concern, the tax base of the welfare states appeared more fragile.

These were all legitimate reasons for anxiety in the waning years of the 'great society' era. But while they account for a certain loss of confidence on the part of the administrative elite, they don't explain the radical transition in attitudes and expectations which has marked our own age. It is one thing to fear that a good system may not be able to maintain itself; it is quite another to lose faith in that system altogether.

CHAPTER THREE

The Unbearable Lightness of Politics

*"A study of the history of opinion is a
necessary preliminary to the emancipation
of the mind."*

—JOHN MAYNARD KEYNES

Nothing, of course, is ever quite as good as we remember.
The social democratic consensus and the welfare institutions of the postwar decades coincided with some of the worst
town planning and public housing of modern times. From
Communist Poland through social democratic Sweden and Labour Britain into Gaullist France and the South Bronx, over-
confident and insensitive planners plastered cities and suburbs
with unlivable and unsightly housing estates. Some of these are

still with us—Sarcelles, a suburb of Paris, bears witness to the haughty indifference of bureaucratic mandarins to the daily life of their subjects. Ronan Point, a peculiarly ugly high-rise in east London, had the good taste to fall down of its own accord but most of the buildings of that era are still with us.

The indifference of local and national authorities to the harm wrought by their decisions can stand for a troubling aspect of postwar planning and renewal. The idea that those in authority know best—that they are engaged in social engineering on behalf of people who do not understand what is good for them—was not born in 1945, but it flourished in the decades that followed. This was the age of Le Corbusier: how the masses felt about their new apartments, the new towns to which they had been moved, the 'quality of life' to which they had been assigned, was all too often a matter of indifference.

By the late 1960s, the idea that "nanny knows best" was already starting to produce a backlash. Middle class voluntary organizations began to protest at the wholesale and abusive clearing not just of 'ugly' slums but also of prized buildings and townscapes: the wanton destruction of New York's Pennsylvania Station and London's Euston Station, the elevation of a monstrous office tower at the heart of Paris's ancient Montparnasse *quartier*, the unimaginative redistricting of whole cities. Rather than an exercise in socially responsible modernization on behalf of the community, these began to appear as symptoms of uncontrolled and insensitive power.

Even in Sweden, where the Social Democrats' grip on office remained as firm as ever, the relentless uniformity of even the best housing projects, social services or public health policies began to grate on a younger generation. Had more people known about the eugenicist practices of some Scandinavian governments in the postwar years, encouraging and even enforcing selective sterilization for the greater benefit of all, the sense of oppressive dependence upon a panoptic state might have been greater still. In Scotland, where the municipally-owned tower blocks of working-class Glasgow housed upwards of 90% of the city's population, their air of dilapidation bore witness to the indifference of municipal (socialist) councils to the condition of their proletarian constituents.

The sense, widespread by the '70s, that the 'responsible' state was unresponsive to the needs and desires of those for whom it spoke contributed to a widening social gulf. On the one hand, there stood an older generation of planners and social theorists. Heirs to the managerialist confidence of the Edwardians, these men and women remained proud of their achievements. Middle-class themselves, they were especially pleased at their success in binding the old elites into a new social order.

But the beneficiaries of that order—whether Swedish shopkeepers, Scottish shipworkers, inner-city African-Americans or bored French suburbanites—were increasingly resentful of their dependence upon administrators, local councilors and bureaucratic regulations. Ironically, it was precisely the middle classes who were most contented with their lot—in large measure because they came into contact with the providential state as a source of popular services rather than as a restriction upon autonomy and initiative.

But the greatest gulf was now the one separating generations. For anyone born after 1945, the welfare state and its institutions were not a solution to earlier dilemmas: they were simply the normal conditions of life—and more than a little dull. The baby boomers, entering university in the mid-'60s, had only ever known a world of improving life chances, generous medical and educational services, optimistic prospects of upward social mobility and—perhaps above all—an indefinable but ubiquitous sense of *security*. The goals of an earlier generation of reformers were no longer of interest to their successors. On the contrary, they were increasingly perceived as restrictions upon the self-expression and freedom of the individual.

THE IRONIC LEGACY OF THE '60S

"My generation of the Sixties, with all our great ideals, destroyed liberalism, because of our excesses."

—CAMILLE PAGLIA

It was a curiosity of the age that the generational split transcended class as well as national experience. The *rhetorical* expression of youthful revolt was, of course, confined to a tiny minority: even in the US in those days, most young people did not attend university and college protests did not necessarily represent youth at large. But the broader symptoms of generational dissidence—music, clothing, language—were unusually widespread thanks to television, transistor radios and the internationalization of popular culture. By the late '60s, the culture gap separating young people from their parents was perhaps greater than at any point since the early 19th century.

This breach in continuity echoed another tectonic shift. For an older generation of left-leaning politicians and voters, the relationship between 'workers' and socialism—between 'the poor' and the welfare state—had been self-evident. The 'Left' had long been associated with—and largely dependent upon—

the urban industrial proletariat. Whatever their pragmatic attraction to the middle classes, the reforms of the New Deal, the Scandinavian social democracies and Britain's welfare state had rested upon the presumptive support of a mass of blue collar workers and their rural allies.

But in the course of the 1950s, this blue collar proletariat was fragmenting and shrinking. Hard graft in traditional factories, mines and transport industries was giving way to automation, the rise of service industries and an increasingly feminized labor force. Even in Sweden, the social democrats could no longer hope to win elections simply by securing a majority of the traditional labor vote. The old Left, with its roots in working class communities and union organizations, could count on the instinctive collectivism and communal discipline (and subservience) of a corralled industrial work force. But that was a shrinking percentage of the population.

The *new* Left, as it began to call itself in those years, was something very different. To a younger generation, 'change' was not to be brought about by disciplined mass action defined and led by authorized spokesmen. Change itself appeared to have moved on from the industrial West into the developing or 'third' world. Communism and capitalism alike were charged with stagnation and 'repression'. The initiative for radical innovation and action now lay either with distant peasants or else with a new set of revolutionary constituents. In place of the male pro-letariat there were now posited the candidacies of 'blacks', 'students', 'women' and, a little later, homosexuals.

Since none of these constituents, at home or abroad, was separately represented in the institutions of welfare societies, the new Left presented itself quite consciously as opposing not merely the injustices of the capitalist order but above all the 'repressive tolerance' of its most advanced forms: precisely those benevolent overseers responsible for liberalizing old constraints or providing for the betterment of all.

Above all, the new Left—and its overwhelmingly youthful constituency—rejected the inherited collectivism of its prede-cessor. To an earlier generation of reformers from Washington to Stockholm, it had been self-evident that 'justice', 'equal op-portunity' or 'economic security' were shared objectives that could only be attained by common action. Whatever the short-comings of over-intrusive top-down regulation and control, these were the price of social justice—and a price well worth paying.

A younger cohort saw things very differently. Social justice no longer preoccupied radicals. What united the '60s genera-tion was not the interest of all, but the needs and rights of each. 'Individualism'—the assertion of every person's claim to maxi-mized private freedom and the unrestrained liberty to express autonomous desires and have them respected and institutionalized by society at large—became the left-wing watchword of the hour. Doing 'your own thing', 'letting it all hang out', 'making love, not war': these are not inherently unappealing goals, but they are of their essence private objectives, not public goods. Unsurprisingly, they led to the widespread assertion that 'the personal is political'.

The politics of the '60s thus devolved into an aggregation of individual claims upon society and the state. 'Identity' began to colonize public discourse: private identity, sexual identity, cultural identity. From here it was but a short step to the fragmentation of radical politics, its metamorphosis into multiculturalism. Curiously, the new Left remained exquisitely sensitive to the collective attributes of humans in distant lands, where they could be gathered up into anonymous social categories like 'peasant', 'post-colonial', 'subaltern' and the like. But back home, the individual reigned supreme.

However legitimate the claims of individuals and the importance of their rights, emphasizing these carries an unavoidable cost: the decline of a shared sense of purpose. Once upon a time one looked to society—or class, or community—for one's normative vocabulary: what was good for everyone was by definition good for anyone. But the converse does not hold. What is good for one person may or may not be of value or interest to another. Conservative philosophers of an earlier age understood this well, which was why they resorted to *religious* language and imagery to justify traditional authority and its claims upon each individual.

But the individualism of the new Left respected neither collective purpose nor traditional authority: it was, after all, both *new* and *left*. What remained to it was the subjectivism of private—and privately-measured—interest and desire. This, in turn, invited a resort to aesthetic and moral relativism: if something is good for me it is not incumbent upon me to ascertain whether it is good for someone else—much less to impose it upon them ("do your own thing").

True, many radicals of the '60s were quite enthusiastic supporters of imposed choices, but only when these affected distant peoples of whom they knew little. Looking back, it is striking to note how many in western Europe and the United States expressed enthusiasm for Mao Tse-tung's dictatorially uniform 'cultural revolution' while defining cultural reform at home as the maximizing of private initiative and autonomy.

In distant retrospect it may appear odd that so many young people in the '60s identified with 'Marxism' and radical projects of all sorts, while simultaneously disassociating themselves from conformist norms and authoritarian purposes. But Marxism was the rhetorical awning under which very different dissenting styles could be gathered together—not least because it offered an illusory continuity with an earlier radical generation. But under that awning, and served by that illusion, the Left fragmented and lost all sense of shared purpose.

On the contrary, 'Left' took on a rather selfish air. To be on the Left, to be a radical in those years, was to be self-regarding, self-promoting and curiously parochial in one's concerns. Left-wing student movements were more preoccupied with college gate hours than with factory working practices; the university-attending sons of the Italian upper-middle-class beat up under-paid policemen in the name of revolutionary justice; light-hearted ironic slogans demanding sexual freedom displaced angry pro-letarian objections to capitalist exploiters. This is not to say that a new generation of radicals was insensitive to injustice or po-litical malfeasance: the Vietnam protests and the race riots of the '60s were not insignificant. But they were divorced from any sense of collective purpose, being rather understood as exten-sions of individual self-expression and anger.

These paradoxes of meritocracy—the '60s generation was above all the successful byproduct of the very welfare states on which it poured such youthful scorn—reflected a failure of nerve. The old patrician classes had given way to a generation of well-intentioned social engineers, but neither was prepared for the radical disaffection of their children. The implicit consensus of the postwar decades was now broken, and a new, decidedly unnatural consensus was beginning to emerge around the primacy of private interest. The young radicals would never have described their purposes in such a way, but it was the distinction between praiseworthy private freedoms and irritating public constraints which most exercised their emotions. And this very distinction, ironically, described the newly emerging Right as well.

THE REVENGE OF THE AUSTRIANS

> *"We must face the fact that the preservation of individual freedom is incompatible with a full satisfaction of our views of distributive justice."*
>
> —FRIEDRICH HAYEK

Conservatism—not to mention the ideological Right—was a minority preference in the decades following World War II. The old, pre-war Right had discredited itself twice over. In the English-speaking world, the conservatives had failed to anticipate, understand or repair the scale of the damage wrought by the Great Depression. By the outbreak of war, only the hard core of the old English Conservative Party and rock-ribbed know-nothing Republicans still opposed the efforts of New Dealers in Washington and semi-Keynesian administrators in London to respond imaginatively to the crisis.

In continental Europe, conservative elites paid the price for their accommodation (and worse) with the occupying powers. With the defeat of the Axis they were swept from office and power. In eastern Europe, the old parties of the center and right were brutally destroyed by their communist successors, but even in western Europe there was no place for traditional reactionaries. A new generation of moderates took their place.

Intellectual conservatism fared little better. For every Michael Oakeshott, embattled in his rigorous contempt for *bien pensant* modern thought, there were a hundred progressive intellectuals making the case for the postwar consensus. No one had much time for free marketeers or 'minimal statists'; and even though most older liberals were still instinctively suspicious of social engineering, they were committed if only on prudential grounds to a very high level of governmental activism. Indeed, the center of gravity of political argument in the years after 1945 lay not between left and right but rather *within* the left: between communists and their sympathizers and the mainstream liberal-social-democratic consensus.

The nearest thing to a serious theoretical conservatism in those consensus years came from men like Raymond Aron in

France, Isaiah Berlin in the UK and—albeit in a rather different key—Sidney Hook in the USA. All three would have blenched at the label 'conservative': they were classic liberals, anti-communist on ethical as well as political grounds and marinated in 19th century suspicion of the over-mighty state. In their different ways, such men were realists: they accepted the need for welfare and social intervention, not to speak of progressive taxation and the collective pursuit of public goods. But by instinct and experience they were opposed to all forms of authoritarian power.

Aron was best known in these years for his unwavering hostility to dogmatic Marxist ideologues and his clear-eyed support for a United States whose shortcomings he never denied. Berlin became famous for his 1958 lecture on "Two Concepts of Liberty", where he distinguished between positive liberty—the pursuit of rights which only a state can guarantee—and negative liberty: the right to be left alone to do as one sees fit. Although he saw himself to the end as a traditional liberal, sympathetic to all of the reformist aspirations of the British liberal tradition with which he identified, Berlin thus emerged as a founding reference for a later generation of neo-libertarians.

Hook, like so many of his American contemporaries, was preoccupied with the anti-Communist struggle. His liberalism thus devolved in practice into an argument for the traditional freedoms of an open society. By conventional US criteria, men like Hook were social democrats in all but name: they shared with other American 'liberals' like Daniel Bell an elective affinity for European political ideas and practices. But the strength of his antipathy to communism opened a bridge between Hook and more conventional conservatives, across which both sides would stride with growing ease in the years to come.

The task of a renascent Right was made easier not just by the passage of time—as people forgot the traumas of the 1930s and '40s, so they were more open to the appeal of traditional conservative voices—but also by their opponents. The narcissism of student movements, new Left ideologues and the popular culture of the '60s generation invited a conservative backlash. We, the Right could now assert, stand for 'values', 'the nation', 'respect', 'authority' and the heritage and civilization of a country—or continent or even 'the West'—for which 'they' (the Left, students, youth, radical minorities) have no understanding or empathy.

We have lived so long with this rhetoric that it seems self-evident the Right would resort to it. But until the mid-'60s or so, it would have been absurd to claim that 'the Left' was insensitive to the nation or traditional culture, much less 'authority'. On the contrary, the old Left was incorrigibly old-fashioned in just these ways. The cultural values of a Keynes or a Reith, a Malraux or a De Gaulle were uncritically shared by many of their leftist opponents: except for a brief moment in the aftermath of the Russian Revolution, the mainstream political Left was as reliably conventional in aesthetics as it was in so much else. If the Right had been constrained to deal exclusively with social democrats and welfare liberals of the older sort, it could never have secured a monopoly of cultural conservatism and 'values'.

Where conservatives *could* point to a contrast between themselves and the old Left was precisely in the matter of the state and its uses. Even here, it was not until the mid-1970s that a new generation of conservatives felt emboldened to challenge the 'statism' of their predecessors and offer radical prescriptions for dealing with what they described as the 'sclerosis' of over-ambitious governments and their deadening impact upon private initiative.

Margaret Thatcher, Ronald Reagan and—far more tentatively—Valéry Giscard d'Estaing in France were the first mainstream right-of-center politicians to risk such a break with the postwar consensus. True, Barry Goldwater in the 1964 presidential election had made an early foray in that direction: but with disastrous consequences. Six years later, Edward Heath—the future Conservative prime minister—experimented with proposals for freer markets and a more restrained state; but he was violently and unfairly castigated for his 'anachronistic' resort to defunct economic ideas and beat a hasty retreat.

As Heath's misstep suggests, while many people were irritated at over-mighty trade unions or insensitive bureaucrats, they were unwilling to countenance a wholesale retreat. The social democratic consensus and its institutional incarnations might be boring and even paternalist; but they worked and people knew it. So long as it was widely believed that the 'Keynesian revolution' had wrought irreversible change, conservatives were stymied. They might win cultural battles over 'values' and 'morals'; but unless they could force public policy debate onto a very different terrain, they were doomed to lose the economic and political war.

The victory of conservatism and the profound transformation brought about over the course of the next three decades was thus far from inevitable: it took an intellectual revolution. In the course of little more than a decade, the dominant 'paradigm' of public conversation shifted from interventionary enthusiasms and the pursuit of public goods to a view of the world best summed up in Margaret Thatcher's notorious *bon mot*: "there is no such thing as society, there are only individuals and families". In the United States, at almost exactly the same moment, Ronald Reagan achieved lasting popularity for his claim that it was "morning in America". Government was no longer the solution—it was the problem.

If government is the problem and society does not exist, then the role of the state is reduced once again to that of facilitator. The task of the politician is to ascertain what is best for the individual, and then afford him the conditions in which to pursue it with minimal interference. The contrast with the Keynesian consensus could not be more glaring: Keynes himself had taken the view that capitalism would not survive if its workings were reduced to merely furnishing the wealthy with the means to get wealthier.

It was precisely such a blinkered understanding of the operations of a market economy which had led, in his view, to the abyss. Why, then, did we in our own times revert to a similar confusion, reducing public conversation to a debate cast in narrowly economic terms? For the Keynesian consensus to be overthrown with such consummate ease and apparent unanimity, the counter-arguments must have been forceful indeed. They were, and they did not come out of nowhere.

We are the involuntary heirs to a debate with which most people are altogether unfamiliar. When asked what lies behind the new (old) economic thinking, we can reply that it was the work of Anglo-American economists associated overwhelmingly with the University of Chicago. But if we ask where the

'Chicago boys' got their ideas, we shall find that the greatest influence was exercised by a handful of foreigners, all of them immigrants from central Europe: Ludwig von Mises, Friedrich Hayek, Joseph Schumpeter, Karl Popper, and Peter Drucker.

Von Mises and Hayek were the outstanding 'grandfathers' of the Chicago school of free-market economics. Schumpeter is best known for his enthusiastic description of the "creative, destructive" powers of capitalism, Popper for his defense of the "open society" and his writings on totalitarianism. As for Drucker, his publications on management exercised enormous influence over the theory and practice of business in the prosperous decades of the postwar boom. Three of these men were born in Vienna, a fourth (von Mises) in Austrian Lemberg (now Lvov), the fifth (Schumpeter) in Moravia, a few dozen miles north of the imperial capital. All five were profoundly shaken by the interwar catastrophe that struck their native Austria.

Following the cataclysm of World War I and a brief socialist municipal experiment in Vienna (where Hayek and Schumpeter joined the debates over economic socialization), the country fell to a reactionary coup in 1934 and then, four years later, to the Nazi invasion and occupation. Like so many others, the young Austrian economists were forced into exile by these events and all—Hayek in particular—were to cast their writings and teachings in the shadow of what became the central question of their lifetime: Why had liberal Austria collapsed and given way to fascism?

Their answer: the unsuccessful attempts of the (Marxist) Left to introduce into post-1918 Austria state-directed planning, municipally owned services, and collectivized economic activity had not only failed; they had led directly to a counter-reaction. Thus Popper, to take the best-known case, argued that the indecision of his socialist contemporaries—paralyzed by their faith in 'historical laws'—was no match for the radical energies of fascists, who *acted*.[13] The problem was that socialists had too much faith in both the logic of history and the reason of men. Fascists, being uninterested in both, were supremely well-placed to step in.

In the eyes of Hayek and his contemporaries, the European tragedy had thus been brought about by the shortcomings of the *Left*: first through its inability to achieve its objectives and then thanks to its failure to withstand the challenge from the Right. Each of them, albeit in different ways, arrived at the same conclusion: the best—indeed the only—way to defend liberalism and an open society was to keep the state out of economic life. If authority was held at a safe distance, if politi-

---

13 Malachi Hacohen, Karl Popper, *The Formative Years, 1902–1945: Politics and Philosophy in Inter-war Vienna* (New York: Cambridge University Press, 2000), p. 379.

cians—however well-intentioned—were barred from planning, manipulating, or directing the affairs of their fellow citizens, then extremists of Right and Left alike would be kept at bay.

The same dilemma—how to understand what had happened between the wars and prevent its recurrence—was confronted by Keynes, as we have seen. Indeed, the English economist asked essentially the same questions as Hayek and his Austrian colleagues. However, for Keynes it had become self-evident that the best defense against political extremism and economic collapse was an *increased* role for the state, including but not confined to countercyclical economic intervention.

Hayek proposed the opposite. In his 1944 classic, *The Road to Serfdom*, he wrote:

> *No description in general terms can give an adequate idea of the similarity of much of current English political literature to the works which destroyed the belief in Western civilization in Germany, and created the state of mind in which naziism could become successful.*[14]

14 Friedrich Hayek, *The Road to Serfdom* (Chicago: University of Chicago Press, 1944), p. 196.

In other words, Hayek—by now living in England and teaching at the London School of Economics—was explicitly projecting (on the basis of Austrian precedent) a fascist outcome should Labour, with its loudly proclaimed welfare and social service objectives, win power in Britain. As we know, Labour did indeed win. But far from paving the way for a revival of fascism, its victory helped stabilize postwar Britain.

In the years following 1945 it seemed to most intelligent observers as though the Austrians had made a simple category error. Like so many of their fellow refugees, they had assumed that the conditions which brought about the collapse of liberal capitalism in interwar Europe were permanent and infinitely reproducible. Thus in Hayek's eyes, Sweden was another country doomed to follow Germany's path into the abyss thanks to the political successes of its Social Democratic governing majority and their ambitious legislative program.

Mis-learning the lessons of Nazism—or assiduously applying a highly selective handful of them—the intellectual refugees from central Europe marginalized themselves in the prosperous postwar West. In the words of Anthony Crosland, writing in 1956 at the height of postwar social democratic confidence, "no one of any standing now believes the once-popular Hayek thesis that any interference with the market mechanism must start us down the slippery slope that leads to totalitarianism."[15]

The intellectual refugees—and especially the economists among them—lived in a condition of endemic resentment toward their uncomprehending hosts. All non-individualist social thought—any argument that rested upon collective categories, common objectives or the notion of social goods, justice, etc.—aroused in them troubling recollections of past upheavals. But even in Austria and Germany circumstances had changed radically: their memories were of little practical application. Men like Hayek or von Mises seemed doomed to professional and cultural marginality. Only when the welfare states whose failure they had so sedulously predicted began to run into difficulties did they once again find an audience for their views: high taxation inhibits growth and efficiency, governmental regulation stifles initiative and entrepreneurship, the smaller the state the healthier the society and so forth.

Thus when we recapitulate conventional clichés about free markets and western liberties, we are in effect echoing—like light from a fading star—a debate inspired and conducted seventy years ago by men born for the most part in the late 19th century. To be sure, the economic terms in which we are en-

15 Anthony Crosland, *op. cit.,* p. 500.

couraged to think today are not usually associated with these far-off political disagreements and experiences. Most students in graduate business schools have never heard of some of these exotic foreign thinkers and are not encouraged to read them. And yet without an understanding of the Austrian origins of their (and our) way of thinking, it is as though we speak a language we do not fully comprehend.

It is perhaps worth noting here that even Hayek cannot be held responsible for the ideological simplifications of his acolytes. Like Keynes, he regarded economics as an interpretive science, not amenable to prediction or precision. If planning was wrong for Hayek, this was because it was obliged to base itself on calculations and predictions which were essentially meaningless and thus irrational. Planning was *not* a moral misstep, much less undesirable on some general principle. It was simply unworkable—and, had he been consistent, Hayek would have acknowledged that much the same applied to 'scientific' theories of the market mechanism.

The difference, of course, was that planning required enforcement if it was to work as intended, and thus led directly to dictatorship—Hayek's real target. The efficient market might be a myth, but at least it did not entail coercion from above. All the same, Hayek's dogmatic rejection of all central control invited the charge of . . . dogmatism. It was Michael

Oakeshott who observed that 'Hayekism' was itself a doctrine: "A plan to resist all planning may be better than its opposite, but it belongs to the same style of politics."[16]

In the United States, among a younger generation of self-confident econometricians (a sub-discipline of whose boastful scientificity both Hayek and Keynes would have had much to say), the belief that democratic socialism is unachievable and has perverse consequences has become something close to a theology. This creed has attached itself to popular condemnation of every effort to increase the role of the state—or the public sector—in the daily lives of American citizens.

In the UK this particular extension of the Austrian lesson has not gained comparable traction. The reasons are obvious— the popularity of free medical care or subsidized higher education to take the best-known examples. But in the course of the Thatcher-Blair-Brown era the sanctification of bankers, brokers, traders, the new rich and anyone with access to large sums of money has led to unstinting admiration for a minimally-regulated 'financial services industry'—and a consequential faith in the naturally benevolent workings of the global market for financial products.

What precisely Hayek or even Schumpeter, the prophet of

16 Michael Oakeshott, *op. cit.*, p. 26.

capitalist destruction, would have made of this crass worship of money and those who have it is another question. But there can be no doubt that what passes for justification of the vast and growing wealth gap in modern Britain derives directly from the apologetics for limited regulation, minimal interference and the virtues of the private sector to which Austrian economic writing contributed so directly.

The British case, even more than the American, points up the practical consequences of this retro-transformation of modern economic language: although the sad story of Icelandic enthusiasms for the wilder shores of bandit banking is more illustrative still. Beginning with a handful of outstanding intellectual refugees from interwar Europe, we pass through two generations of academic economists intent on re-configuring their discipline . . . and arrive at the banking, mortgage, private finance and hedge fund scandals of recent years.

Behind every cynical (or merely incompetent) banking executive and trader sits an economist, assuring them (and us) from a position of unchallenged intellectual authority that their actions are publicly useful and should in any case not be subject to collective oversight. Behind that economist and his gullible readers there stand in turn participants in long-dead debates. The etiolated condition of our present public language—our inability to think our way beyond the categories and clichés that shape and distort policy-making in Washington and London alike—thus pays homage to one of Keynes's greatest insights:

> *Practical men, who believe themselves to be quite exempt from any intellectual influences, are usually the slaves of some defunct economist. Madmen in authority, who hear voices in the air, are distilling their frenzy from some academic scribbler of a few years back. I am sure that the power of vested interests is vastly exaggerated compared with the gradual encroachment of ideas.[17]*

THE CULT OF THE PRIVATE

> *"To suggest social action for the public good to the city of London is like discussing The Origin of Species with a Bishop sixty years ago."*
>
> —JOHN MAYNARD KEYNES

So what have Keynes's 'madmen in authority' done with the ideas they inherited from defunct economists? They have set about dismantling the properly *economic* powers and initiatives of the state. It is important to be clear: this in no way

---

17 Quoted in Robert Skidelsky, *John Maynard Keynes: Volume 2: The Economist as Savior, 1920–1937* (New York: Penguin, 1995), p. 570.

entailed reducing the state *per se*. Margaret Thatcher, like George W. Bush and Tony Blair after her, never hesitated to augment the repressive and information-gathering arms of central government. Thanks to CCTV cameras, wiretapping, Homeland Security, the UK's Independent Safeguarding Authority and other devices, the panoptic control that the modern state can exercise over its subjects has continued to expand. Whereas Norway, Finland, France, Germany and Austria—all of them 'cradle-to-grave' nanny states—have never resorted to such measures except in wartime, it is the liberty-vaunting Anglo-Saxon market societies that have gone farthest in these Orwellian directions.

Meanwhile, if we had to identify just one general consequence of the intellectual shift that marked the last third of the 20th century, it would surely be the worship of the private sector and, in particular, the cult of privatization. Some might say that the enthusiasm for dispensing with publicly-owned goods was purely pragmatic. Why privatize? Because, in an age of budgetary constraints, privatization appears to save money. If the state owns an inefficient factory or a costly service—a waterworks, say, or a railway—it offloads it onto private buyers.

The sale duly earns money for the state. Meanwhile, by entering the private sector, the operation in question becomes more efficient thanks to the workings of the profit motive. Everyone

benefits: the service improves, the state rids itself of an inappro-
priate responsibility, investors profit, and the public sector makes
a one-time gain from the sale. On the face of it, then, privatization
represents a retreat from dogmatic state-centered preferences and
a turn towards straightforwardly economic calculations.

After all, "[t]he performance of nationalized industries in
almost every country has not been demonstrably better than that
of private or mixed categories."[18] And there can be no doubt of
the downsides of public ownership. In the UK especially, the
Treasury regarded potentially profitable operations as mere cash
cows. There was to be a minimum of investment and a maximum of profit-taking to augment the public coffers. Thus railways and coal mines were expected to hold their prices down for
social and political reasons; but at the same time, they were required to turn a profit.

In the long run, this made for inefficient operations. Elsewhere, in Sweden for example, the state was less heavy-handed
in its economic manipulation, but often regulated wages, conditions, prices and products to deadening effect. And so, in addition to the short-term cash benefits of privatization there was
added the hypothetical gain in initiative and efficiency. If noth-

18 Daniel Bell, *The Cultural Contradictions of Capitalism* (New York: Basic Books,
1976), p. 275.

ing else, it was reasonably assumed, a business that reverted from public ownership to private hands would surely be run with a view to long-term investment and efficient pricing.

So much for the theory. The practice has been very different. With the advent of the modern state (notably over the course of the past century), transport, hospitals, schools, mails, armies, prisons, police forces and affordable access to culture—essential services not well served by the workings of the profit motive— were taken under public regulation or control. They are now being handed back to private entrepreneurs.

What we have been watching is the steady shift of public responsibility onto the private sector to no discernible collective advantage. Contrary to economic theory and popular myth, privatization is *inefficient*. Most of the things that governments have seen fit to pass into the private sector were operating at a loss: whether they were railway companies, coal mines, postal services, or energy utilities, they cost more to provide and maintain than they could ever hope to attract in revenue.

For just this reason, such public goods were inherently unattractive to private buyers unless offered at a steep discount. But when the state sells cheap, the public takes a loss. It has been calculated that, in the course of the Thatcher-era UK privatizations, the deliberately low price at which long-standing public assets were marketed to the private sector resulted in a net transfer of £14 billion from the taxpaying public to stockholders and other investors.

To this loss should be added a further £3 billion in fees to the bankers who transacted the privatizations. Thus the state in effect paid the private sector some £17 billion ($30 billion) to facilitate the sale of assets for which there would otherwise have been no takers. These are significant sums of money—approximately the endowment of Harvard University, for example, or the annual gross domestic product of Paraguay or Bosnia-Herzegovina. This can hardly be construed as an efficient use of public resources.

One reason that privatization in the United Kingdom appears misleadingly beneficial is that it correlates positively with the end of decades of decline relative to Britain's European competitors. But this outcome was achieved almost wholly as a result of falling growth rates elsewhere: there was no sudden upturn in British economic performance. The best study of UK privatizations concludes that privatization per se had a decidedly modest impact upon long-term economic growth—while regressively redistributing wealth from taxpayers and consumers to the shareholders of newly privatized companies.[19]

The only reason that private investors are willing to purchase

---

19 Massimo Florio, *The Great Divestiture: Evaluating the Welfare Impact of the British Privatizations 1979–1997* (Cambridge: The MIT Press, 2006), p. 342.

apparently inefficient public goods is because the state eliminates or reduces their exposure to risk. In the case of the London Underground, for example, a 'Public-Private Partnership' (PPP) was set up to invite interested investors to buy into the Tube network. The purchasing companies were assured that whatever happened they would be protected against serious loss—thereby undermining the economic case for privatization: the workings of the profit motive. Under these privileged conditions, the private sector will prove at least as inefficient as its public counterpart—creaming off profits and charging losses to the state.

The outcome has been the worst sort of 'mixed economy': individual enterprise indefinitely underwritten by public funds. In Britain, newly-privatized National Health Service Hospital Groups periodically fail—typically because they are encouraged to make all manner of profits but forbidden to charge what they think the market might bear. At this point the hospital Trusts (like the London Underground, whose PPP collapsed in 2007) turn back to the government to pick up the bill. When this happens on a serial basis—as it did with the nationalized railways— the effect is creeping *de facto* re-nationalization with none of the benefits of public control.[20]

---

20 In its last year of operation, 1994, state-owned British Rail cost the taxpayer £950 million ($1.5 billion). By 2008, Network Rail, its semiprivate successor company, cost taxpayers £5 billion ($7.8 billion).

The result is moral hazard. The popular cliché that the bloated banks which brought international finance to its knees in 2008 were 'too big to fail' is of course infinitely extendable. No government could permit its railway system simply to 'fail'. Privatized electric or gas utilities, or air traffic control networks, cannot be allowed to grind to a halt through mismanagement or financial incompetence. And, of course, their new managers and owners know this.

Curiously, this point escaped the otherwise sharp eye of Friedrich Hayek. In his insistence that monopolistic industries (including railways and utilities) be left in private hands, he neglected to foresee the implications: since such vital national services would never be allowed to collapse, they could take risks, misspend or misappropriate resources at will, and always know that the government would pick up the tab.

Moral hazard even applies in the case of institutions and businesses whose operations are in principle beneficial to the collectivity. Recall the case of Fannie Mae and Freddie Mac, the private agencies responsible for providing mortgages to middle class Americans: a service vital to the wellbeing of a consumer economy founded on property ownership and cheap loans. For some years before the 2008 debacle, Fannie Mae had been borrowing money from the government (at artificially depressed interest rates) and lending it commercially at a very substantial profit.

Since the company was private (though with privileged access to public funds), those profits constituted public monies recycled to the company's shareholders and executives. The fact that millions of mortgages were made available as a result of these self-interested transactions merely compounds the crime: when Fannie Mae was forced to call in its loans, it spread suffering across a huge swathe of the American middle class.

Americans have privatized less than their British admirers. But the deliberate under-funding of unloved public services like Amtrak has resulted in an inadequate facility doomed sooner or later to be offered at knock-down prices to a private buyer. In New Zealand, where the government privatized its rail and ferry services in the course of the 1990s, their new owners mercilessly stripped away all marketable assets. In July 2008, the government in Wellington reluctantly took the sadly eviscerated and still unprofitable transport operations back into public control—at far greater expense than would have been needed to invest in them properly in the first place.

There are winners as well as losers in the privatization story. In Sweden, following a banking crisis that left the state severely short of revenue, the (conservative) government of the early '90s re-allocated 14% of the country's hitherto state-monopolized pension contributions from the public system to private retirement accounts. Predictably, the chief beneficiary of this shift was the country's insurance companies. In the same way, the terms under which British utilities were sold to the highest bidder included the 'pre-pensioning' of tens of thousands of workers. The workers lost their jobs, the state was saddled with an un-funded pension burden—but the shareholders of the new private utility companies were relieved of all responsibility.

Shifting the ownership onto businessmen allows the state to relinquish moral obligations. This was quite deliberate: in the UK between 1979 and 1996 (i.e., in the Thatcher and Major years) the private sector share of personal services contracted out by government rose from 11% to 34%, with the sharpest increase in residential care for the elderly, children and the mentally ill. Newly privatized homes and care centers naturally reduced the quality of service to the minimum in order to increase profits and dividends. In this way, the welfare state was stealthily unwound to the advantage of a handful of entrepreneurs and shareholders.

'Contracting out' brings us to the third and perhaps most telling case against privatization. Many of the goods and services that states seek to divest have been badly run: incompetently managed, underinvested, etc. Nevertheless, however poorly run, postal services, railway networks, retirement homes, prisons, and other provisions targeted for privatization cannot be left entirely to the vagaries of the market. They are, in the overwhelming majority of cases, inherently the sort of activity that *someone* has to regulate—that is why they ended up in public hands in the first place.

This semiprivate, semipublic disposition of essentially collective responsibilities returns us to a very old story indeed. If your tax returns are audited in the US today, this is because the *government* has decided to investigate you; but the investigation itself will very likely be conducted by a *private* company. The latter has contracted to perform the service on the state's behalf, in much the same way that private agents have contracted with Washington to provide security, transportation, and technical know-how (at a profit) in Iraq and Afghanistan.

Governments, in short, now increasingly farm out their responsibilities to private firms that offer to administer them better than the state and at a savings. In the 18th century this was called tax farming. Early modern governments often lacked the means to collect taxes and thus invited bids from private individuals to undertake the task. The highest bidder would get the job, and was free—once he had paid the agreed sum—to collect whatever he could and retain the proceeds. The government took a discount on its anticipated tax revenue, in return for cash up front.

After the fall of the monarchy in France, it was widely conceded that tax farming is absurdly inefficient. In the first place, it discredits the state, represented in the popular mind by a grasping private profiteer. Secondly, it generates considerably less revenue than a well-administered system of government collection, if only because of the profit margin accruing to the private collector. And thirdly, you get disgruntled taxpayers.

In the US and the UK today, we have a discredited state and a glut of grasping private profiteers. Interestingly, we do not (yet) have disgruntled taxpayers—or, at least, they are typically disgruntled for the wrong reasons. Nevertheless, the problem we have created for ourselves is essentially comparable to that which faced the *ancien régime*.

As in the 18th century, so today: by eviscerating the state's responsibilities and capacities, we have undermined its public standing. Few in England and fewer still in America continue to believe in what was once thought of as a 'public service mission': the duty to provide certain sorts of goods and services just because they are in the public interest. A government that acknowledges its reluctance to assume such responsibilities, preferring to shift them to the private sector and leave them to the vagaries of the market, may or may not be contributing to efficiency. But it is abandoning core attributes of the modern state.

In effect, privatization reverses a centuries-long process

whereby the state took on things that individuals could not or would not do. The corrosive consequences of this for public life are, as so often, rendered inadvertently explicit in the new 'policy-speak'. In English higher educational circles today, the market-as-metaphor dominates conversation. Deans and heads of departments are constrained to assess 'output' and economic 'impact' when judging the quality of someone's work. When English politicians and civil servants bother to justify the abandonment of traditional public service monopolies, they talk of 'diversifying providers'. When the UK Work and Pensions Secretary announced plans in June 2008 to privatize social services—including short-term palliative welfare-to-work schemes which enable Whitehall to publish misleadingly low unemployment figures—he described himself as 'optimizing welfare delivery'.

What does it mean to those on the receiving end when everything from the local bus service to the regional parole officer are now part of some private company which measures their performance with exclusive reference to short-term profitability? In the first place, there is a negative welfare impact (to use the term of art). The chief shortcoming of the old public services was the restrictive regulations and facilities—one-size-fits-all—with which they were notoriously associated: Swedish alcohol outlets, British Railways cafes, unionized French welfare offices and so forth. But at least their provision was universal, and for good and ill they were regarded as a public responsibility.

The rise of enterprise culture has destroyed all that. It may suit a privatized telephone company to provide polite, automated call centers to attend to complaints (whereas under the old nationalized arrangements, complainants were under no illusions that anyone was listening); but nothing substantive improves. Moreover, a social service provided by a private company does not present itself as a collective good to which all citizens have a right. Unsurprisingly, there has been a sharp falling off in the number of people claiming benefits and services to which they are legally entitled.

The result is an eviscerated society. From the point of view of the person at the bottom—seeking unemployment pay, medical attention, social benefits or other officially mandated services—it is no longer to the state, the administration or the government that he or she instinctively turns. The service or benefit in question is now often 'delivered' by a private intermediary. As a consequence, the thick mesh of social interactions and public goods has been reduced to a minimum, with nothing except authority and obedience binding the citizen to the state.

This reduction of 'society' to a thin membrane of interactions between private individuals is presented today as the ambition of libertarians and free marketeers. But we should never forget that it was first and above all the dream of Jacobins, Bolsheviks and Nazis: if there is nothing that binds us together as a community or society, then we are utterly dependent upon the state. Governments that are too weak or discredited to act through their citizens are more likely to seek their ends by other means: by exhorting, cajoling, threatening and ultimately coercing people to obey them. The loss of social purpose articulated through public services actually *increases* the unrestrained powers of the over-mighty state.

There is nothing mysterious about this process: it was well described by Edmund Burke in his critique of the French Revolution. Any society, he wrote in *Reflections on the Revolution in France*, which destroys the fabric of its state, must soon be "disconnected into the dust and powder of individuality". By eviscerating public services and reducing them to a network of farmed-out private providers, we have begun to dismantle the fabric of the state. As for the dust and powder of individuality: it resembles nothing so much as Hobbes's war of all against all, in which life for many people has once again become solitary, poor and more than a little nasty.

THE DEMOCRATIC DEFICIT

*"We differ from other states in regarding the man
who holds aloof from public life as useless."*

—PERICLES

O ne striking consequence of the disintegration of the public sector has been an increased difficulty in compre-
hending what we have in common with others. We are familiar
with complaints about the 'atomizing' impact of the internet: if
everyone selects gobbets of knowledge and information that
interest them, but avoids exposure to anything else, we do indeed form global communities of elective affinity—while losing touch with the affinities of our neighbors.

In that case, what is it that binds us together? Students frequently tell me that they only know and care about a highly
specialized subset of news items and public events. Some may
read of environmental catastrophes and climate change. Others
are taken up by national political debates but quite ignorant of
foreign developments. In the past, thanks to the newspaper
they browsed or the television reports they took in over dinner,
they would at least have been 'exposed' to other matters. Today,
such extraneous concerns are kept at bay.

This problem highlights a misleading aspect of globalization. Young people are indeed in touch with likeminded persons many thousands of miles away. But even if the students of Berkeley, Berlin and Bangalore share a common set of interests, these do not translate into *community*. Space matters. And politics is a function of space—we vote where we live and our leaders are restricted in their legitimacy and authority to the place where they were elected. Real-time access to likeminded fellows half a world away is no substitute.

Think for a minute about the importance of something as commonplace as an insurance card or pension book. Back in the early days of the welfare states, these had to be regularly stamped or renewed in order for their possessor to collect her pension, food stamps or child allowance. These rituals of exchange between the benevolent state and its citizens took place at fixed locations: a post office, typically. Over time, the shared experience of relating to public authority and public policy— incarnated in these services and benefits—contributed mightily to a tauter sense of shared citizenship.

This sentiment was crucial to the formation of modern states and the peaceful societies they governed. Until the late 19th century, government was simply the apparatus by which an inherited ruling class exercised power. But little by little, the state took upon itself a multitude of tasks and responsibilities hitherto in the hands of individuals or private agencies.

Examples abound. Private security agencies were replaced (and disbanded) in favor of national or municipal police forces. Private mail services were made redundant by the development of national post offices. Mercenaries were forced out of business, replaced by national conscript armies. Private transportation services did not disappear—retreating instead into luxury provisions for the very wealthy—but were displaced as the primary means of communication by publicly-owned or regulated buses, trams, trolleys and trains. The patronage system of artistic support—well adapted to private operas for independent princelings and isolated courts—was steadily displaced (though never entirely) by publicly-funded arts, supported by national and local taxation and administered by state agencies.

The point can be extended indefinitely. The emergence of national football (soccer) leagues across Europe served simultaneously to channel popular energies, forge local identities and establish a nation-wide sense of space and shared enthusiasms. Much like France's famous turn-of-the-century geography text, *Le Tour de la France par deux enfants*, which socialized a generation of French schoolchildren into an appreciation of the map of France, so the formation of the Football Leagues in England and Scotland introduced young fans to the geography of their country through the competition of teams from its various regions.

From its early years through the 1970s, the Football League was always a single entity: 'meritocratic' in the sense that teams could rise or fall through its various divisions according to their performance. Footballers, recruited locally, wore the colors of their team. Such advertising as there was confined itself to placards mounted around the pitch; the idea of attaching commercial announcements to the players themselves would simply never have occurred to anyone—the resulting cacophony of colour and text would have detracted from the visual unity of the team.

Indeed, visual representations of collective identity used to matter a lot. Think of the black London taxi, its distinctive monotone emerging by consensus between the wars and serving thereafter to distinguish not only the taxis themselves but something about the austere unity of the city they served. Buses and trains followed suit, their uniformity of color and design emphasizing the role they played as common transporters of a single people.

The same purpose may be ascribed in retrospect to the distinctively British enthusiasm for school uniforms (not unknown elsewhere, but usually associated with religious or communitarian identity—parochial schools, for example). Looking back across the chasm which opened up with the 'individualist' enthusiasms of the '60s, it is hard for us today to appreciate their virtues. Surely, we now suppose, such dress codes stifle the identity and personality of the young?

Rigid dress codes can indeed enforce authority and suppress individuality—an army uniform is intended to do just that. But in their time, uniforms—whether worn by schoolchildren, mailmen, train conductors or street-crossing wardens—bespoke a certain egalitarianism. A child in regulation clothing is under no pressure to compete sartorially with his better-off contemporaries. A uniform makes identification with others, across social or ethnic boundaries, involuntary and thus—in the end— natural.

Today, to the extent that we even acknowledge shared social obligations and claims, these are characteristically met in private. The mails are increasingly beleaguered by the private delivery services which cream off profitable business, leaving the Post Office to subsidize costly delivery and collection services for the poor and in remote areas. Buses and trains are in private hands, festooned with advertisements and garishly decorated in loud colours that announce the identity of their owners rather than the service they provide. The arts—in Britain or Spain, for example—are funded by the proceeds of privately administered lotteries, raising money from the poorer members of the community through the encouragement of legalized gambling.

Football Leagues across Europe have devolved into ultra-wealthy Super Leagues for a handful of privileged clubs, with the remainder mired in their poverty and irrelevance. The idea of a 'national' space has been replaced by international competition underwritten by ephemeral foreign funders, their coffers recouped from commercial exploitation of players recruited from afar and unlikely to remain in place very long.

London's taxis, once famous for their efficient design and the astonishing local knowledge of their drivers, now come in myriad colors. In the latest retreat from functional uniformity, non-conventional makes and models are permitted to advertise themselves as official taxis—even though they can neither perform the hitherto mandatory turning circles nor meet long-established load capacities. Within a predictable future, we may expect the famous 'knowledge'—the intimate familiarity with London's maze of streets and squares required of every licensed taxi driver since 1865—to be abandoned or diluted in the name of free enterprise.

Armies, especially the American army, are increasingly dependent for logistical support, material provision and transportation security upon private services—the latter furnished at great expense by companies hiring mercenaries on short-term contract: at the last count, 190,000 'auxiliary' private employees were 'assisting' the US armed forces in Iraq and Afghanistan.

The police once incarnated the modern state's ambition to regulate social intercourse and monopolize authority and violence. Less than two centuries after their first appearance, they are being displaced by private security companies whose function it is to serve and secure the 'gated communities' that have sprung up in our cities and suburbs over the past three decades.

What exactly is a 'gated community' and why does it matter? In its initial American usage—now enthusiastically applied in parts of London and elsewhere across Europe, as well as throughout Latin America and in wealthy Asian entrepots from Singapore to Shanghai—the term denotes people who have gathered together into affluent subdivisions of suburbs and cities and fondly suppose themselves functionally independent of the rest of society.

Before the rise of the modern state, such communities were commonplace. If they were not actually fortified in practice, they certainly represented a distinct private space, its boundaries well-marked and secured against outsiders. As modern cities and nation states grew up, so these fortified enclaves—often owned by a single aristocrat or limited private company –blended into the urban surroundings. Their inhabitants, confident in the security now offered to them by the public authorities, abandoned their private police forces, dismantled their fences and confined their exclusivity to distinctions of wealth and status. As recently as the 1960s, their reappearance in our midst would have seemed quite bizarre.

But today, they are everywhere: a token of 'standing', a shameless acknowledgment of the desire to separate oneself from other members of society, and a formal recognition of the state's (or the city's) inability or unwillingness to impose its authority across a uniform public space. In America one typically finds gated communities in far-flung suburbs. But in England as elsewhere, they have sprung up at the heart of the city.

'Stratford City', in east London, covers some 170 acres and claims the power to control all activity in the (public) streets under its jurisdiction. 'Cabot Circus' in Bristol, 'Highcross' in Leicester, 'Liverpool One' (which spans 34 streets and is owned by Grosvenor, the Duke of Westminster's property company) are all privately-owned and privately-controlled spaces at the heart of what were once public municipalities. They reserve the right to impose a range of restrictions and regulations according to taste: no skateboarding, no rollerblading, no eating in certain locations, no begging, no vagrancy, no photographs and of course a myriad of private security and closed circuit cameras to enforce the above.

A moment's reflection reveals the contradiction of such parasitic communities-within-the-community. The private security firms they hire are not entitled by law to act in the name of the state and must thus call upon the police to assist them in the event of serious crime. The streets they purport to own and maintain were initially surveyed, built, paved and lit at public expense: so today's privatized citizens are the undeserving beneficiaries of yesterday's taxpayers. The public highways that allow members of a gated community to travel freely between home and work were also provided—and are still maintained—by society at large, as are the public services (schools, hospitals, post offices, fire engines and the like) on which 'gated citizens' may call with the same rights and expectations as their un-privileged neighbors.

It is claimed on their behalf that gated communities act as a bulwark against violations of their members' liberties. People are safer within their gates and pay for the privilege; they are free to live among their own. Accordingly, they can insist upon rules and regulations with respect to décor, design and deportment that reflect their 'values' and which they do not seek to impose on non-members beyond their gates. But in practice these excessive exercises in the 'privatization' of daily life actually fragment and divide public space in a way that threatens everyone's liberty.

The contemporary impulse to live in such private spaces with people like oneself is not confined to wealthy property owners. It is the same urge that drives African-American or

Jewish students in colleges today to form separate 'houses', to eat apart and even to learn primarily about themselves by enrolling in identity studies majors. But in universities, like society at large, such self-protective undertakings not only starve their beneficiaries of access to a broader range of intellectual or public goods, they fragment and diminish the experience of everyone.

People who live in private spaces contribute actively to the dilution and corrosion of the public space. In other words, they exacerbate the circumstances which drove them to retreat in the first place. And by so doing, they pay a price. If public goods—public services, public spaces, public facilities—are devalued, diminished in the eyes of citizens and replaced by private services available against cash, then we lose the sense that common interests and common needs ought to trump private preferences and individual advantage. And once we cease to value the public over the private, surely we shall come in time to have difficulty seeing just why we should value law (*the* public good par excellence) over force.

In recent years the idea that law should always have precedence over force has fallen into disuse: were it otherwise, we should not so readily have signed on for a 'preventive' war in defiance of all international legal opinion. To be sure, this is a matter of foreign policy, an arena in which realism has often trumped allegiance to treaty or the recognition of law. But how long will it be before we import such criteria into our domestic arrangements?

In an age when young people are encouraged to maximize self-interest and self-advancement, the grounds for altruism or even good behavior become obscured. Short of reverting to religious authority—itself on occasion corrosive of secular institutions—what can furnish a younger generation with a sense of purpose beyond its own short-term advantage? The late Albert Hirschman spoke of the "liberating experience" of a life directed to action on the public behalf: "[t]he greatest asset of public action is its ability to satisfy vaguely felt needs for higher purpose and meaning in the lives of men and women, especially of course in an age in which religious fervor is at a low ebb in many countries".[21]

One of the moderating constraints of the '60s was the widespread impulse to enter public service or the liberal professions: education, medicine, journalism, government, the arts or public sector law. Few—very few—graduates before the mid-'70s sought out a 'business' education; and the numbers applying to law school were far lower than they are today. In-

---

21 Albert O. Hirschman, *Shifting Involvements: Private Interest and Public Action* (Princeton, NJ: Princeton University Press, 1982), p. 126.

strumental self-advancement conflicted with the acquired habit of working with and for one's fellow citizens.

If we don't respect public goods; if we permit or encourage the privatization of public space, resources and services; if we enthusiastically support the propensity of a younger generation to look exclusively to their own needs: then we should not be surprised to find a steady falling-away from civic engagement in public decision-making. In recent years there has been much discussion of the so-called 'democratic deficit'. The steadily declining turnout at local and national elections, the cynical distaste for politicians and political institutions consistently register in public opinion polls—most markedly among the young. There is a widespread sense that since 'they' will do what they want in any case—while feathering their own nests—why should 'we' waste time trying to influence the outcome of their actions.

In the short-run, democracies can survive the indifference of their citizens. Indeed, it used to be thought an indication of impending trouble in a well-ordered republic when electors were too much aroused. The business of government, it was widely supposed, should be left to those elected for the purpose. But the pendulum has swung far in the opposite direction.

The turnout in American presidential and congressional elections has long been worryingly low and continues to fall. In the United Kingdom, parliamentary elections—once an occasion for widespread civic engagement—have seen a steady decline in participation since the 1970s: to take an exemplary case, Margaret Thatcher won more votes in her first electoral victory than on any subsequent occasion. If she continued to triumph, it was because the opposition vote fell even faster. The European Union parliamentary elections, inaugurated in 1979, are notorious for the low numbers of European citizens who bother to turn out.

Why does this matter? Because—as the Greeks knew—participation in the way you are governed not only heightens a collective sense of responsibility for the things government does, it also keeps our rulers honest and holds authoritarian excess at bay. Political demobilization, beyond the healthy retreat from ideological polarization which characterized the growth of political stability in postwar western Europe, is a dangerous and slippery slope. It is also cumulative: if we feel excluded from the management of our collective affairs, we shall not bother to speak up about them. In that case, we should not be surprised to discover that no one is listening to us.

The danger of a democratic deficit is always present in systems of indirect representation. Direct democracy, in small political units, enhances participation—though with the attendant risk of conformity and majoritarian oppression: there is nothing as potentially repressive of dissent and difference as a town hall meeting or a kibbutz. Choosing people to speak for us at some distant assembly is a reasonable mechanism for balancing the representation of interests in large and complex communities. But unless we mandate our representatives to say only what we have authorized—an approach favored by radical students and revolutionary crowds—we are constrained to allow them to follow their own judgment.

The men and women who dominate western politics today are overwhelmingly products—or, in the case of Nicolas Sarkozy, byproducts—of the '60s. Bill and Hillary Clinton, Tony Blair and Gordon Brown are all 'baby boomers'. So are Anders Fogh Rasmussen, the 'liberal' prime minister of Denmark; Ségolène Royal and Martine Aubry, the bickering challengers for leadership of France's anemic Socialist Party and Herman Van Rompuy, the worthy but underwhelming new President of the European Union.

This cohort of politicians have in common the enthusiasm that they fail to inspire in the electors of their respective countries. They do not seem to believe very firmly in any coherent set of principles or policies; and though none of them—with the possible exception of Blair—is as execrated as former president George W. Bush (another baby boomer), they form a striking contrast to the statesmen of the World War II generation. They convey neither conviction nor authority.

Beneficiaries of the welfare states whose institutions they call into question, they are all Thatcher's children: politicians who have overseen a retreat from the ambitions of their predecessors. Few—once again, with the exception of Bush and Blair—could be said actively to have betrayed the democratic trust placed in them. But if there is a generation of public men and women who share responsibility for our collective suspicion of politics and politicians, they are its true representatives. Convinced that there is little they can do, they do little. The best that might be said of them, as so often of the baby boom generation, is that they stand for nothing in particular: politicians-lite.

No longer trusting in such persons, we lose faith not just in parliamentarians and congressmen, but in Parliament and Congress themselves. The popular instinct at such moments is either to 'throw the rascals out' or else leave them to do their worst. Neither of these responses bodes well: we don't know how to throw them out and we can no longer afford to let them do their worst. A third response—'overthrow the system!'—is discredited by its inherent inanity: which bits of which system and in favor of which systemic substitute? In any case, who will do the overthrowing?

We no longer have political movements. While thousands of us may come together for a rally or march, we are bound together on such occasions by a single shared interest. Any effort to convert such interests into collective goals is usually undermined by the fragmented individualism of our concerns. Laudable goals—fighting climate change, opposing war, advocating public healthcare or penalizing bankers—are united by nothing more than the expression of emotion. In our political as in our economic lives, we have become consumers: choosing from a broad gamut of competing objectives, we find it hard to imagine ways or reasons to combine these into a coherent whole. We must do better than this.

CHAPTER FOUR

Goodbye to All That?

"Finding a homeland is not the same as dwelling in the place where our ancestors once used to live."

—Krzysztof Czyzewski

When Communism fell in 1989, the temptation for Western commentators to gloat triumphantly proved irresistible. This, it was declared, marked the end of History. Henceforth, the world would belong to liberal capitalism— there was no alternative—and we would all march forward in unison towards a future shaped by peace, democracy and free markets. Twenty years on this assertion looks threadbare.

There can be no question that the fall of the Berlin Wall and the domino-like collapse of Communist states from the suburbs of Vienna to the shores of the Pacific marked a very significant transition: one in which millions of men and women were liberated from a dismal and defunct ideology and its authoritarian institutions. But no one could credibly assert that what replaced Communism was an era of idyllic tranquility. There was no peace in post-Communist Yugoslavia, and precious little democracy in any of the successor states of the Soviet Union.

As for free markets, they surely flourished, but it is not clear for whom. The West—Europe and the United States above all—missed a once-in-a-century opportunity to re-shape the world around agreed and improved international institutions and practices. Instead, we sat back and congratulated ourselves upon having won the Cold War: a sure way to lose the peace. The years from 1989 to 2009 were consumed by locusts.

1989 AND THE END OF THE LEFT

"The worst thing about Communism is what comes after."

—ADAM MICHNIK

With Communism there fell more than just a handful of repressive states and a political dogma. The disappearance of so many regimes so closely bound to a revolutionary narrative marked the death knell of a 200-year promise of radical progress. In the wake of the French Revolution, and with growing confidence following Lenin's seizure of power in 1917, the Marxist Left had been intimately associated with the claim that not only *should* a socialist future displace the capitalist present, but that it *must* assuredly do so. In the skeptical words of the philosopher Bernard Williams, the Left simply took it for granted that the goals it sought "... are being cheered on by the universe".[22]

It is hard today to recall this secular faith—the absolute certainty with which intellectuals and radical politicians invoked inexorable 'historical' laws to justify their political be-

---

22 Bernard Williams, *Philosophy as a Humanistic Discipline* (Princeton, NJ: Princeton University Press, 2006), p. 144.

liefs. One source was 19th century positivism: neo-scientific self-confidence in the political uses of social data. On October 24th, 1884, the young Beatrice Webb describes herself in her diary as toying with facts, rolling them between her fingers as she tried ". . . to imagine that before me lies a world of knowledge wherewith I may unite the knots of human destiny."[23] As William Beveridge would later comment, people like the Webbs ". . . gave one the sense that by taking sufficient thought one could remedy all the evils in the world, by reasoned progress."[24]

This late Victorian confidence was hard-pressed to survive the 20th century. By the 1950s, it was already shaken in many quarters by the crimes committed on History's behalf by Lenin and his successors: according to the late Ralf Dahrendorf, Richard Tawney (the British social historian who died in 1962) was ". . . the last person whom I heard speak about progress without an apparent sense of embarrassment".[25]

Nevertheless, at least until 1989 it remained possible in principle to believe that history moved in certain ascertainable directions and that—for good or ill—Communism represented the culmination of one such trajectory: the fact that this is an

---

23 Beatrice Webb, *My Apprenticeship* (London: Longmans, Green and Co., 1926), p. 137.
24 José Harris, *William Beveridge: A Biography* (Oxford: The Clarendon Press, 1977), p. 119.
25 Ralf Dahrendorf, *op. cit.,* p. 124.

essentially religious notion did not detract from its appeal to generations of secular progressives. Even after the disillusionment of 1956 and 1968, there were still many who clung to political allegiances that placed them on the 'correct' side of the future, however troubling the present.

One especially important feature of this illusion was the enduring attraction of Marxism. Long after Marx's prognoses had lost all relevance, many social democrats as well as Communists continued to insist—if only *pro forma*—on their fidelity to the Master. This loyalty provided the mainstream political Left with a vocabulary and a range of fall-back doctrinal first principles; but it deprived that same Left of practical political responses to real-world dilemmas.

During the slump and the depression of the '30s, many self-styled Marxists refused to propose or even debate solutions to the crisis. Like old-fashioned bankers and neo-classical economists, they believed that capitalism has laws that cannot be bent or broken and that there was no point in interfering in its workings. This unyielding commitment rendered many socialists, then and for years to come, unsympathetic to moral challenges: politics, they asserted, are not about rights or even justice. They are about class, exploitation and forms of production.

Thus, socialists and social democrats alike remained to the end in thrall to the core presuppositions of 19th century socialist thought. This residual belief system—its relationship to genuine ideology being roughly that of English low-church Anglicanism to full-blown Catholic orthodoxy—provided a back wall against which anyone calling themselves a social democrat could lean their policies and thereby distinguish themselves from even the most reform-oriented liberal or Christian Democrat.

That is why the fall of Communism mattered so much. With its collapse, there unraveled the whole skein of doctrines which had bound the Left together for over a century. However perverted the Muscovite variation, its sudden and complete disappearance could not but have a disruptive impact on any party or movement calling itself 'social democratic'.

This was a peculiarity of left-wing politics. Even if every conservative and reactionary regime around the globe were to implode tomorrow, its public image hopelessly tarnished by corruption and incompetence, the politics of conservatism would survive intact. The case for 'conserving' would remain as viable as it ever had been. But for the Left, the absence of a historically-buttressed narrative leaves an empty space. All that remains is politics: the politics of interest, the politics of envy, the politics of re-election. Without idealism, politics is reduced to a form of social accounting, the day-to-day administration of men and things. This too is something that a conservative can survive well enough. But for the Left it is a catastrophe.

From the outset, the democratic Left in Europe saw itself as the reasonable alternative to revolutionary socialism and—in later years—to its Communist successor. Social democracy was thus inherently schizophrenic. While marching confidently forward into a better future, it was constantly glancing nervously over its left shoulder. *We*, it seemed to say, are not authoritarian. *We* are for freedom, not repression. *We* are democrats who also believe in equality, social justice and regulated markets.

So long as the primary aim of social democrats was to convince voters that they were a respectable radical choice within the liberal polity, this defensive stance made sense. But today such rhetoric is incoherent. It is not by chance that a Christian Democrat like Angela Merkel can win an election in Germany against her Social Democratic opponents—even at the height of a financial crisis—with a set of policies that in all its important essentials resembles their own program.

Social democracy, in one form or another, is the prose of contemporary European politics. There are very few European politicians, and fewer still in positions of influence, who would dissent from core social democratic assumptions about the duties of the state, however much they might differ as to their scope.

Consequently, social democrats in today's Europe have nothing distinctive to offer: in France, for example, even their disposition to favor state ownership hardly distinguishes them from the Colbertian instincts of the Gaullist right. The problem today lies not in social democratic policies, but in their exhausted language. Since the authoritarian challenge from the left has lapsed, the emphasis upon "democracy" is largely redundant. We are all democrats today.

The Ironies of Post-Communism

"[W]e achieved everything, but for me it turns out that what we achieved satirized what we had dreamt about."

—Krzysztof Kieślowksi

B ut if we are all 'democrats', what now distinguishes us? What do we stand for? We know what we do not want: from the bitter experience of the past century we have learned that there are things that states most certainly should *not* be doing. We have survived an age of doctrines purporting with alarming confidence to say how our rulers should act and to remind individuals—forcibly if necessary—that those in authority know what is good for them. We cannot return to all that.

Conversely, and despite the purported 'lessons' of 1989, we know that the state is not *all* bad. The only thing worse than too much government is too little: in failed states, people suffer at least as much violence and injustice as under authoritarian rule, and in addition their trains do not run on time. Moreover, if we give the matter a moment's thought, we can see that the 20th century morality tale of 'socialism vs. freedom' or 'communism vs. capitalism' is misleading. Capitalism is not a political system; it is a form of economic life, compatible in practice with right-wing dictatorships (Chile under Pinochet), left-wing dictatorships (contemporary China), social-democratic monarchies (Sweden) and plutocratic republics (the United States). Whether capitalist economies thrive best under conditions of freedom is perhaps more of an open question than we like to think.

Conversely, communism—while clearly inimical to a genuinely free market—can apparently adapt to a variety of economic arrangements, though it inhibits the efficiency of all of them. Thus we were correct to suppose that the fall of communism put an end to over-confident claims on behalf of planning and central control; but it is not clear what other conclusions we should draw. And it simply does not follow that communism's failure discredited all state provision or economic planning.

The real problem facing us in the aftermath of 1989 is not what to think of communism. The vision of total social organization—the fantasy which animated utopians from Sydney Webb to Lenin, from Robespierre to Le Corbusier—lies in ruins. But the question of how to organize ourselves for the common benefit remains as important as ever. Our challenge is to recover it from the rubble.

As anyone who has traveled or lived in post-Communist eastern Europe will know, the transition from repressive egalitarianism to unconstrained greed is not attractive. There is no shortage of people in the region today who would enthusiastically second the view that the point of political freedom is to make money. Certainly this is the view of President Václav Klaus of the Czech Republic, and he is not alone.

But why should the sight of a handful of greedy businessmen doing well out of the collapse of an authoritarian state be so much more pleasing to our eyes than authoritarianism itself? Both suggest something profoundly amiss in a society. Freedom is freedom. But if it leads to inequality, poverty and cynicism, then we should say so rather than sweep its shortcomings under the rug in the name of the triumph of liberty over oppression.

By the end of the 20th century, social democracy in Europe

had fulfilled many of its longstanding policy objectives, but largely forgotten or abandoned its original rationale. From Scandinavia to Canada, the political Left and the institutions it inaugurated rested on 'cross class' alliances of workers and farmers, blue collar workers and the middle class. It is the defection of the latter that poses the greatest challenge to the welfare states and the parties that had brought them into being. Despite being the chief beneficiaries of welfare legislation in much of Europe and North America, the growing share of western electorates that identified with the 'middle' was increasingly skeptical and resentful of the tax burden imposed on it in order to maintain egalitarian institutions.

The growth in unemployment over the course of the 1970s added to the strain on the public exchequer and lowered its tax revenue. Moreover, the inflation of those years increased the tax and insurance burden—if only nominally—upon those still employed. Since the latter were disproportionately better skilled and educated, they came to resent this. What had once been implicitly accepted as a reciprocal arrangement came to be described as 'unfair': the benefits of the welfare state were now 'excessive'.

Whereas in the 1940s the majority of manual workers paid no tax and were thus net beneficiaries of the new social benefits, by the 1970s—once again thanks to inflation as well as wage increases—many of them had entered middle class tax brackets. Moreover, with the passage of time, they had retired—and were thus drawing benefits in the form of pensions and age-related public provisions (free bus passes, subsidized performances at theaters and concert halls). These were now being paid for by their children, who had no first-hand memory of the Depression and the war and thus no direct familiarity with the circumstances that had given rise to these provisions. They just resented their cost.

From a pessimistic perspective, the social democratic 'moment' thus failed to outlast its founding generation. As the beneficiaries aged and memory faded, the appeal of expensive *états providentiaux* waned accordingly. This process accelerated over the course of the '80s and '90s as the neo-liberal regimes of the age selectively taxed universal benefits: a surreptitious re-introduction of the means test that was calculated to diminish middle class enthusiasm for social services now perceived as benefiting only the very poor.

Are social democracy and welfare states insupportably expensive? Much has been made of the apparently absurd provisions for early retirement on near-full pay from which many European public sector workers now benefit—at substantial and unpopular cost to private sector taxpayers. One well-known instance concerns train drivers in France, entitled to retire in their fifties on a generous and inflation-protected pension. How, critics ask, can any efficient economy survive such burdens?

When (Communist-dominated) rail unions negotiated these packages shortly after the Second World War, the railwaymen were a very different class of worker. Typically recruited straight from school at the age of thirteen, they had been doing dangerous manual work—operating steam engines—for upwards of four decades. By retirement in their early fifties, they were exhausted: often sick and with a life expectancy rarely in excess of ten years. Generous pensions were the least they could reasonably ask, and the burden on the state was easily tolerated.

Today's TGV drivers spend their working day comfortably ensconced in a warm (or air-conditioned) cab, and the nearest they come to manual labor is when they press a series of electric switches to activate their machinery. For them to retire before the age of fifty-five appears absurd. It is certainly expensive: thanks to the medical and other provisions of the French welfare state, such men may reasonably expect to live well into their eighties. This places a significant burden upon the public finances, as well as on the annual budget of the state railways.

But the answer is not to abolish the principle of generous retirement packages, medical provision and other welfare goods. Politicians need to find the courage to insist (in this case) upon a significant raising of the retirement age—and then justify themselves to their constituents. But such changes are unpopular, and politicians today eschew unpopularity at almost any cost. To a very considerable extent, the dilemmas and shortcomings of the welfare state are a result of political pusillanimity rather than economic incoherence.

Nonetheless, the problems facing social democracy are real. Without an ideological narrative, and shorn of its self-described 'core' constituencies, it has become something of an orphan in the wake of the euphoric delusions of post-'89. And few can deny that welfarism, taken to extremes, carries a whiff of do as you're told!: there were moments in postwar Scandinavia when the enthusiasm for eugenics and social efficiency suggested not just a certain insensitivity to recent history but also to the natural human desire for autonomy and independence.

Moreover, as Leszek Kołakowski once observed, the welfare state entails protecting the weak majority from the strong and privileged minority. Reasonable as it sounds, this principle is implicitly undemocratic and potentially totalitarian. But social democracy has never descended into authoritarian rule. Why? Is it democratic institutions that keep politicians honest? More likely, it was the deliberately inconsistent application of the logic of the protective state which preserved its democratic form.

Unfortunately, pragmatism is not always good politics. The greatest asset of mid-20th century social democracy—its willingness to compromise its own core beliefs in the name of balance, tolerance, fairness and freedom—now looks more like weakness: a loss of nerve in the face of changed circumstances. We find it hard to look past those compromises to recall the qualities that informed progressive thought in the first place: what the early 20th century syndicalist Edouard Berth termed "a revolt of the spirit against . . . a world in which man was threatened by a monstrous moral and metaphysical materialism".

WHAT HAVE WE LEARNED?

"No great improvements in the lot of mankind are possible, until a great change takes place in the fundamental constitution of their modes of thought."

—JOHN STUART MILL

What, then, *should* we have learned from 1989? Perhaps, above all, that nothing is either necessary or inevitable. Communism did not have to happen—and there was no reason why it should last forever; but nor had we any grounds for being confident that it would fall. Progressives must take onboard the sheer contingency of politics: neither the rise of the welfare states nor their subsequent fall from grace should be treated as a gift from History. The social democratic 'moment'—or its American counterpart from the New Deal to the Great Society—was the product of a very particular combination of circumstances unlikely to repeat themselves. The same can be said of the neo-liberal 'moment' which began in the 1970s and has only now run itself into the ground.

But precisely because history is not foreordained, we mere mortals must invent it as we go along—and in circumstances, as old Marx rightly pointed out, not entirely of our own making. We shall have to ask the perennial questions again, but be open to different answers. We need to sort out to our own satisfaction what aspects of the past we wish to keep and what made them possible. Which circumstances were unique? And which circumstances could we, with sufficient will and effort, reproduce?

If 1989 was about re-discovering liberty, what limits are we now willing to place upon it? Even in the most 'freedom-loving' societies, freedom comes with constraints. But if we accept some limitations—and we always do—why not others? Why are we so sure that some planning, or progressive taxation, or the collective ownership of public goods, are intolerable restrictions on liberty; whereas closed-circuit television cameras, state bailouts for investment banks 'too big to fail', tapped telephones and expensive foreign wars are acceptable burdens for a free people to bear?

There may be good answers to these questions; but how can we know unless we pose them? We need to rediscover how to talk about change: how to imagine very different arrangements for ourselves, free of the dangerous cant of 'revolution'. We must distinguish better than some of our predecessors between desirable ends and unacceptable means. At the very least, we should accommodate Keynes's warning on this matter: "[i]t is not sufficient that the state of affairs which we seek to promote should be better than the state of affairs which preceded it; it must be sufficiently better to make up for the evils of the transition."[26]

But having acknowledged and digested all of these considerations, we need to look ahead: what do we want and why do we want it? As the present dilapidated condition of the Left suggests, the answers are not self-evident. But what alternative do we have? We can hardly put the past behind us and merely keep our fingers crossed: we know from experience that politics, like nature, abhors a vacuum. After twenty wasted years it is time to start again. What is to be done?

---

26 John Maynard Keynes, *Two Memoirs—Dr. Melchior, a Defeated Enemy and My Early Beliefs* (New York: A. M. Kelly, 1949), p. 156.

.

CHAPTER FIVE

What Is to Be Done?

*"I think that Capitalism, wisely managed,
can probably be made more efficient for
attaining economic ends than any
alternative system yet in sight. But that
in itself is in many ways extremely
objectionable. Our problem is to work
out a social organization which shall be
as efficient as possible without offending
our notions of a satisfactory way of life."*

—JOHN MAYNARD KEYNES

Those who assert that 'the system' is at fault, or who see mysterious maneuverings behind every political misstep, have little to teach us. But the disposition to disagree, to reject and to dissent—however irritating it may be when taken to extremes—is the very lifeblood of an open society. We need people who make a virtue of opposing mainstream opinion. A democracy of permanent consensus will not long remain a democracy.

The Case for Dissent

"Instead of using their vastly increased material and technical resources to build a wonder city, the men of the nineteenth century built slums . . . [which] on the test of private enterprise, 'paid,' whereas the wonder city would, they thought, have been an act of foolish extravagance, which would, in the imbecile idiom of the financial fashion, have 'mortgaged the future' . . . The same rule of self-destructive financial calculation governs every walk of life. We destroy the beauty of the countryside because the un-appropriated splendors of nature have no economic value. We are capable of shutting off the sun and the stars because they do not pay a dividend."

—John Maynard Keynes

It is tempting to conform: community life is a lot easier where everyone appears to agree with everyone else, and where dissent is blunted by the conventions of compromise. Societies and communities where these are absent or have broken down do not fare well. But there is a price to be paid for conformity. A closed circle of opinion or ideas into which discontent or opposition is never allowed—or allowed only within circumscribed and stylized limits—loses its capacity to respond energetically or imaginatively to new challenges.

The United States is a country founded upon small communities. As anyone who has lived for any length of time in such places can attest, the natural instinct is always to impose a regulative uniformity upon members' public behavior. In the US, this disposition is partly countered by the individualistic propensities of the early settlers and the constitutional protections they prescribed for minority and individual dissent. But the balance, noted by Alexis de Tocqueville among many others, has long since swung towards conformity. Individuals remain free to say what they wish; but if their opinions cut athwart those of the majority they will find themselves outcast. At the very least the impact of their words will be muted.

Britian used to be different: a traditional monarchy governed by a hereditary elite which preserved its hold on power by permitting and even incorporating dissent and advertising its tolerance as a virtue. But the country has become less elitist and more populist; the non-conformist streak in public life has been steadily disqualified—as Tocqueville might have predicted. Today, full-blooded dissent from received opinion on everything from political correctness to tax rates is almost as uncommon in the UK as in the United States.

There are many sources of non-conformity. In religious societies, particularly those with an established faith—Catholicism, Anglicanism, Islam, Judaism—the most effective and enduring dissident traditions are rooted in theological differences: it is not by chance that the British Labour Party was born in 1906 from a coalition of organizations and movements which drew heavily on non-conformist congregations. Class distinctions too are a fertile breeding ground for dissident sentiments. In class-divided societies (or, occasionally, in communities organized by caste) those at the bottom are strongly motivated to protest their condition and, by extension, the social arrangements that perpetuate it.

In more recent decades, dissidence has been closely associated with intellectuals: a class of person first identified with late-19th century protests against the abuse of state power but in our own time better known for speaking and writing against the grain of public opinion. Sadly, contemporary intellectuals have shown remarkably little informed interest in the nitty-gritty of public policy, preferring to intervene or protest on ethically-defined topics where the choices seem clearer. This has left debates on the way we ought to govern ourselves to policy specialists and 'think tanks', where unconventional opinion rarely finds a place and the public are largely excluded.

The problem is not whether we agree or disagree on any given piece of legislation. The problem is the way we debate our shared interests. To take an obvious (because familiar) instance: any conversation here in the United States on the subject of public expenditure and the benefits or otherwise of an active role for government will very quickly fall foul of two exclusion clauses. The first mandates that we are all in favor of holding taxes to the minimum and 'keeping government out of our affairs' wherever possible. The second, in effect a demagogic variation on the first, asserts that none of us would wish to see 'socialism' replace our well-oiled and long-established way of government and life.

Europeans fondly suppose themselves less conformist than Americans. They smile at the religious corrals into which so many US citizens retreat, abandoning independence of mind to group-speak. They point to the perverse consequences of local referenda in California, where well-financed ballot initiatives have destroyed the tax base of the world's seventh largest economy.

But it was a recent referendum in Switzerland that banned the construction of minarets in a country that boasts just four and where almost every resident Muslim is a secular Bosnian

refugee. And it is the British who have meekly accepted everything from closed circuit television cameras to enhanced and
intrusive policing in what is now the world's most 'over-
informed' and authoritarian democracy. There are many respects in which Europe today is a better place than the
contemporary US; but it is far from being perfect.

Even intellectuals have bent the knee. The Iraq war saw the
overwhelming majority of British and American public commentators abandon all pretense at independent thought and toe
the government line. Criticism of the military and those in political authority—always harder in times of war—was pushed
to the margins and treated as something akin to treason. Continental European intellectuals were freer to oppose the gadarene
rush, but only because their own leaders were ambivalent and
their societies divided. The moral courage required to hold a
different view and to press it upon irritated readers or unsympathetic listeners remains everywhere in short supply.

But at least war, like racism, offers clear moral choices. Even
today, most people know what they think about military action
or racial prejudice. But in the arena of economic policy, the citizens of today's democracies have learned altogether too much
modesty. We have been advised that these are matters for experts: that economics and its policy implications are far beyond
the understanding of the common man or woman—a point of

view enforced by the increasingly arcane and mathematical language of the discipline.

Not many 'lay people' are likely to challenge the Chancellor of the Exchequer, the Secretary of the Treasury or their expert advisors in such matters. Were they to do so, they would be told—much as a medieval priest might have advised his flock—that these are questions with which they need not concern themselves. The liturgy must be chanted in an obscure tongue, accessible only to the initiated. For everyone else, faith will suffice.

But faith has *not* sufficed. The emperors of economic policy in Britain and the US, not to mention their acolytes and admirers everywhere from Tallinn to Tbilisi, are naked. However, since most observers have long shared their sartorial preferences, they are ill-placed to object. We need to re-learn how to criticize those who govern us. But in order to do so with credibility we have to liberate ourselves from the circle of conformity into which we, like they, are trapped.

Liberation is an act of the will. We cannot hope to reconstruct our dilapidated public conversation—no less than our crumbling physical infrastructure—unless we become sufficiently angry at our present condition. No democratic state should be able to make illegal war on the basis of a deliberate lie and get away with it. The silence surrounding the contemptibly inadequate response of the Bush Administration to Hurricane Katrina bespeaks a depressing cynicism towards the responsibilities and capacities of the state: we expect Washington to under-perform. The recent US Supreme Court decision permitting unlimited corporate expenditure on election candidates—and the 'expenses' scandal in the UK Parliament—illustrate the uncontrolled role of money in politics today.

Prime Minister Gordon Brown, responding to a January 2010 report on economic inequality in the UK which confirmed the scandalous gap separating rich and poor that his party had done so much to exacerbate, pronounced it "sobering" and conceded that there was "much further to go". One is reminded of Captain Renault in *Casablanca:* "I'm shocked, shocked".

Meanwhile, the precipitous fall from grace of President Obama, in large measure thanks to his bumbling stewardship of health care reform, has further contributed to the disaffection of a new generation. It would be easy to retreat in skeptical disgust at the incompetence (and worse) of those currently charged with governing us. But if we leave the challenge of radical political renewal to the existing political class—to the Blairs and Browns and Sarkozys, the Clintons and Bushes and (I fear) the Obamas—we shall only be further disappointed.

Dissent and dissidence are overwhelmingly the work of the

young. It is not by chance that the men and women who initiated the French Revolution, like the reformers and planners of the New Deal and postwar Europe, were distinctly younger than those who had gone before. Rather than resign themselves, young people are more likely to look at a problem and demand that it be solved.

But they are also more likely than their elders to be tempted by apoliticism: the idea that since politics is so degraded in our time, we should give up on it. There have indeed been occasions where 'giving up on politics' was the right *political* choice. In the last decades of the Communist regimes of eastern Europe, 'anti-politics', the politics of 'as if' and mobilizing 'the power of the powerless' all had their place. That is because official politics in authoritarian regimes are a front for the legitimization of naked power: to bypass them is a radically disruptive political act in its own right. It forces the regime to confront its limits—or else expose its violent core.

However, we must not generalize from the special case of heroic dissenters in authoritarian regimes. Indeed, the example of the 'anti-politics' of the '70s, together with the emphasis on human rights, has perhaps misled a generation of young activists into believing that, conventional avenues of change being hopelessly clogged, they should forsake political organization for single-issue, non-governmental groups unsullied by compromise. Consequently, the first thought that occurs to a young person seeking a way to 'get involved' is to sign up with Amnesty International or Greenpeace, Human Rights Watch or Doctors Without Borders.

The moral impulse is unimpeachable. But republics and democracies exist *only* by virtue of the engagement of their citizens in the management of public affairs. If active or concerned citizens forfeit politics, they thereby abandon their society to its most mediocre and venal public servants. The British House of Commons today is a sad sight: a parlor of placemen, yes-men and professional camp followers—at least as bad as it was in 1832, the last time it was forcibly overhauled and its 'representatives' expelled from their sinecure. The US Senate, once a bulwark of republican constitutionalism, has declined to a pretentious, dysfunctional parody of its original self. The French National Assembly does not even aspire to the status of an approval stamp for the country's president, who bypasses it at will.

During the long century of constitutional liberalism, from Gladstone to LBJ, Western democracies were led by a distinctly superior class of statesmen. Whatever their political affinities, Léon Blum and Winston Churchill, Luigi Einaudi and Willy Brandt, David Lloyd George and Franklin Roosevelt represented a political class deeply sensitive to its moral and social responsibilities. It is an open question as to whether it was the circumstances that produced the politicians, or the culture of the age that led men of this caliber to enter politics. Today, neither incentive is at work. Politically speaking, ours is an age of the pygmies.

And yet that is all we have. Elections to Parliament, congressional elections and the choice of National Assembly members are still our only means for converting public opinion into collective action under law. So young people must not abandon faith in our political institutions. When youthful radicals in 1960s West Germany lost all respect for the Federal Republic and the *Bundestag* (Parliament), they formed "extra-parliamentary action groups": forerunners of the directionless terrorism of the Baader-Meinhoff Gang.

Dissent must remain within the law and seek its goals through political channels. But this is not an argument for passivity or compromise. The institutions of the republic have been degraded, above all by money. Worse, the language of politics itself has been vacated of substance and meaning. A majority of adult Americans are not happy with the way they are governed, with the way decisions are taken and with the undue influence exercised by special interests. In the UK, opinion polls suggest that disillusion with the politicians, the party machines and their policies has never been greater. We would be ill-advised to ignore such sentiments.

The democratic failure transcends national boundaries. The embarrassing fiasco of the Copenhagen climate conference of December 2009 is already translating into cynicism and despair among young people: what is to become of them if we do not take seriously the implications of global warming? The healthcare débâcle in the United States and the financial crisis have accentuated a sentiment of helplessness among even well-disposed voters. We need to act upon our intuitions of impending catastrophe.

RECASTING PUBLIC CONVERSATION

"Without knowledge of wind and current, without some sense of purpose, men and societies do not keep afloat for long, morally or economically, by bailing out the water."

—RICHARD TITMUSS

Most critics of our present condition start with institutions. They look at parliaments, senates, presidents, elections and lobbies and point to the ways in which these have degraded or abused the trust and authority placed in them. Any reform, they conclude, must begin here. We need new laws, different electoral regimes, restrictions on lobbying and political funding; we need to give more (or less) authority to the executive branch and we need to find ways to make elected and unelected officials responsive and answerable to their constituencies and paymasters: us.

All true. But such changes have been in the air for decades. It should by now be clear that the reason they have not happened, or do not work, is because they are imagined, designed and implemented by the very people responsible for the dilemma. There is little point in asking the US Senate to reform its lobbying arrangements: as Upton Sinclair famously observed a century ago, "It is difficult to get a man to understand something when his salary depends on his not understanding it." For much the same reasons, the parliaments of most European countries—now regarded with sentiments ranging from boredom to contempt—are ill-placed to find within themselves the means to become relevant once again.

We need to start somewhere else. Why, for the past three decades, has it been so easy for those in power to convince their constituents of the wisdom—and, in any case, the necessity—of the policies they want to pursue? Because there has been no coherent alternative on offer. Even when there are significant policy differences among major political parties, these are presented as versions of a single objective. It has become commonplace to assert that we all want the same thing, we just have slightly different ways of going about it.

But this is simply false. The rich do not want the same thing as the poor. Those who depend on their job for their livelihood do not want the same thing as those who live off investments and dividends. Those who do not need public services—because they can purchase private transport, education and protection—do not seek the same thing as those who depend exclusively on the public sector. Those who benefit from war—either as defense contractors or on ideological grounds—have different objectives than those who are against war.

Societies are complex and contain conflicting interests. To assert otherwise—to deny distinctions of class or wealth or influence—is just a way to promote one set of interests above another. This proposition used to be self-evident; today we are encouraged to dismiss it as an incendiary encouragement to class hatred. In a similar vein, we are encouraged to pursue economic self-interest to the exclusion of all else: and indeed, there are many who stand to gain thereby.

However, markets have a natural disposition to favor needs and wants that can be reduced to commercial criteria or economic measurement. If you can sell it or buy it, then it is quantifiable and we can assess its contribution to (quantitative) measures of collective well-being. But what of those goods which humans have always valued but which do not lend themselves to quantification?

What of well-being? What of fairness or equity (in its original sense)? What of exclusion, opportunity—or its absence—or lost hope? Such considerations mean much more to most people than aggregate or even individual profit or growth. Take humiliation: what if we treated it as an economic cost, a charge to society? What if we decided to 'quantify' the harm done when people are shamed by their fellow citizens as a condition of receiving the mere necessities of life?

In other words, what if we factored into our estimates of

productivity, efficiency, or well-being the difference between a humiliating handout and a benefit as of right? We might conclude that the provision of universal social services, public health insurance, or subsidized public transportation was actually a cost-effective way to achieve our common objectives. I readily concede that such an exercise is inherently contentious: how do we quantify 'humiliation'? What is the measurable cost of depriving isolated citizens of access to metropolitan resources? How much are we willing to pay for a good society?

Even 'wealth' itself cries out for redefinition. It is widely asserted that steeply progressive rates of taxation or economic redistribution destroy wealth. Such policies undoubtedly constrict the resources of some to the benefit of others—though the way we cut the cake has little bearing on its size. If redistributing material wealth has the long-term effect of improving the health of a country, diminishing social tensions born of envy or increasing and equalizing everyone's access to services hitherto preserved for the few, is not that country better off?[27]

As the reader may observe, I am using words like 'wealth' or 'better off' in ways that take them well beyond their current, strictly material application. To do this on a broader scale—to

---

27 Fred Hirsch, *The Social Limits to Growth* (Cambridge: Harvard University Press, 1976), p.66, note 19.

recast our public conversation—seems to me the only realistic way to begin to bring about change. If we do not talk differently, we shall not think differently.

There are precedents for this way of conceiving political change. In late-18th century France, as the old regime tottered, the most significant developments on the political scene came not in the movements of protest or the institutions of state which sought to head them off. They came, rather, in the very language itself. Journalists and pamphleteers, together with the occasional dissenting administrator or priest, were forging out of an older language of justice and popular rights a new rhetoric of public action.

Unable to confront the monarchy head-on, they set about depriving it of legitimacy by imagining and expressing objections to the way things were and positing alternative sources of authority in whom 'the people' could believe. In effect, they invented modern politics: and in so doing quite literally discredited everything that had gone before. By the time the Revolution itself broke out, this new language of politics was thoroughly in place: indeed, had it not been, the revolutionaries themselves would have had no way to describe what they were doing. In the beginning was the word.

Today, we are encouraged to believe in the idea that politics reflects our opinions and helps us shape a shared public space.

Politicians talk and we respond—with our votes. But the truth is quite other. Most people don't feel as though they are part of any conversation of significance. They are told what to think and how to think it. They are made to feel inadequate as soon as issues of detail are engaged; and as for general objectives, they are encouraged to believe that these have long since been determined.

The perverse effects of this suppression of genuine debate are all around us. In the US today, town hall meetings and 'tea parties' parody and mimic the 18th century originals. Far from opening debate, they close it down. Demagogues tell the crowd what to think; when their phrases are echoed back to them, they boldly announce that they are merely relaying popular sentiment. In the UK, television has been put to strikingly effective use as a safety valve for populist discontent: professional politicians now claim to listen to *vox populi* in the form of instant phone-in votes and popularity polls on everything from immigration policy to pedophilia. Twittering back to their audience its own fears and prejudices, they are relieved of the burden of leadership or initiative.

Meanwhile, across the Channel in republican France or tolerant Holland, *ersatz* debates on national identity and criteria for citizenship substitute for the political courage required to confront popular prejudice and the challenges of integration. Here too, a 'conversation' appears to be taking place. But its terms of reference have been carefully pre-determined; its purpose is not to encourage the expression of dissenting views but to suppress them. Rather than facilitate public participation and diminish civic alienation, these 'conversations' simply add to the widespread distaste for politicians and politics. In a modern democracy it is possible to fool most of the people most of the time: but at a price.

We need to re-open a different sort of conversation. We need to become confident once again in our own instincts: if a policy or an action or a decision seems somehow wrong, we must find the words to say so. According to opinion polls, most people in England are apprehensive about the helter-skelter privatization of familiar public goods: utilities, the London Underground, their local bus service and the regional hospital, not to mention retirement homes, nursing services and the like. But when they are told that the purpose of such privatizations has been to save public money and improve efficiency, they are silent: who could dissent?

THE SOCIAL QUESTION REOPENED

"[E]very man is a piece of the Continent, a part of the Main."

—JOHN DONNE

We face today two practical dilemmas. The first can be succinctly described as the return of the 'social question'. For Victorian reformers—or American activists of the pre-1914 age of reform—the challenge posed by the social question of their time was straightforward: how was a liberal society to respond to the poverty, overcrowding, dirt, malnutrition and ill health of the new industrial cities? How were the working masses to be brought into the community—as voters, as citizens, as participants—without upheaval, protest and even revolution? What should be done to alleviate the suffering and injustices to which the urban working masses were now exposed and how was the ruling elite of the day to be brought to see the need for change?

The history of the 20th century West is in large measure the history of efforts to answer these questions. The responses proved spectacularly successful: not only was revolution avoided but the industrial proletariat was integrated to a remarkable degree. Only in countries where any liberal reform was prevented by authoritarian rulers did the social question rephrase itself as a political challenge, typically ending in violent confrontation. In the middle of the 19th century, sharp-eyed observers like Karl Marx had taken it for granted that the only way the inequities of industrial capitalism could be overcome was by revolution. The idea that they could be dissolved peacefully into New Deals, Great Societies and welfare states simply never would have occurred to him.

However, poverty—whether measured by infant mortality, life expectancy, access to medicine and regular employment or simple inability to purchase basic necessities—has increased steadily since the 1970s in the US, the UK and every country that has modeled its economy upon their example. The pathologies of inequality and poverty—crime, alcoholism, violence and mental illness—have all multiplied commensurately. The symptoms of social dysfunction would have been immediately recognizable to our Edwardian forebears. The social question is back on the agenda.

We should be careful when discussing such matters to avoid purely negative measures. As William Beveridge, the great English reformer, once observed, the risk in describing and addressing 'social problems' lies in reducing them to things like 'drink' or the need for 'charity'. The real issue, for Beveridge as for us, is "... something wider—simply the question of under what conditions it is possible and worthwhile for men as a whole to live."[28] By this he meant that we have to decide what the state must do in order for men and women to pursue decent lives. Merely providing a welfare floor below which people need not sink does not suffice.

The second dilemma we face concerns the social consequences of technological change. These have been with us for some 200 years, ever since the onset of the industrial revolution. With each technical advance, men and women are put out of work, their skills redundant. However, the steady expansion of capitalism ensured new forms of employment—though not always at comparable wage rates and often with reduced status. Together with mass education and universal literacy—achieved in most developed countries over the course of the century 1870-1970—new jobs in new industries making new things for new markets sufficed to ensure a steady improvement in the standard of living of most people.

Today, the situation has changed. Unskilled and semi-skilled work is fast disappearing, not just thanks to mechanized or robotized production but also because the globalization of the labor market favors the most repressive and low-wage

28 José Harris, *op. cit.*, p. 73.

economies (China above all) over the advanced and more egalitarian societies of the West. The only way that the developed
world can respond competitively is by exploiting its compara-
tive advantage in capital-intensive advanced industries where
knowledge counts for everything.

In such circumstances the demand for new skills vastly out-
paces our capacity to teach them—and those skills are anyway
overtaken within a few years, leaving even the best-trained employee in the dust. Mass unemployment—once regarded as a
pathology of badly managed economies—is beginning to look
like an endemic characteristic of advanced societies. At best, we
can hope for 'under-employment'—where men and women
work part-time; accept jobs far below their skill level; or else
undertake unskilled work of the sort traditionally assigned to
immigrants and the young.

The likely consequences of this coming age of uncertainty—
when a growing number of people will have good reason to fear
job loss and long-term redundancy—will be a return to depen-
dency upon the state. Even if it is the private sector that under-
takes retraining schemes, part-time work projects and other
palliative exercises, these programs will be subsidized by the
public sector—as they already are in a number of western countries. No private employer takes on labor as an act of charity.

Even so, the growing number of people who will have good

reason to feel superfluous to the economic life of their society cannot help but pose a serious social challenge. As we have seen, our present approach to welfare provision encourages the view that those who cannot secure regular work are in some measure responsible for their own misfortune. The more such people we have in our midst, the greater the risks to civic and political stability.

A NEW MORAL NARRATIVE?

"Greek ethical thought rested on an objective teleology of human nature, believing that there were facts about man and his place in the world which determined, in a way discoverable to reason, that he was meant to lead a co-operative and ordered life. Some version of this belief has been held by most ethical outlooks subsequently; we are perhaps more conscious now of having to do without it than anyone has been since some fifth-century Sophists first doubted it."

—BERNARD WILLIAMS

The Left has failed to respond effectively to the financial crisis of 2008—and more generally to the shift away from the state and towards the market over the past three decades.

Shorn of a story to tell, social democrats and their liberal and Democratic fellows have been on the defensive for a generation, apologizing for their own policies and altogether unconvincing when it comes to criticizing those of their opponents. Even when their programs are popular, they have trouble defending them against charges of budgetary incontinence or governmental interference.

So what is to be done? What sort of political or moral framework can the Left propose to explain its objectives and justify its goals? There is no longer a place for the old-style master narrative: the all-embracing theory of everything. Nor can we retreat to religion: whatever we think of accounts of God's purposes and His expectations of men, the fact is that we cannot hope to rediscover the kingdom of faith. In the developed world especially, there are fewer and fewer people for whom religion is either a necessary or sufficient motive for public or private action.

Conversely, the fact that many in the West would be perplexed to learn that a public policy was being justified on theological grounds should not blind us to the importance of moral purpose in human affairs. Debates about war, abortion, euthanasia, torture; disputes over public expenditure on health or education: these and so much else are instinctively couched in terms that draw quite directly on traditional religious or philosophical writings, even if these are unfamiliar to contemporary commentators.

It is the gap between the inherently ethical nature of public decision-making and the utilitarian quality of contemporary political debate that accounts for the lack of trust felt towards politics and politicians. Liberals are too quick to mock the bland ethical nostrums of religious leaders, contrasting them with the complexity and seduction of modern life. The remarkable appeal of the late Pope John Paul II to young people inside and outside the Catholic faith should give us pause: humans need a language in which to express their moral instincts.

To put it slightly differently: even if we concede that there is no higher purpose to life, we need to ascribe meaning to our actions in a way that transcends them. Merely asserting that something is or is not in our material interest will not satisfy most of us most of the time. To convince *others* that something is right or wrong we need a language of ends, not means. We don't have to believe that our objectives are poised to succeed. But we do need to be able to believe in them.

Political skepticism is the source of so many of our dilemmas. Even if free markets worked as advertised, it would be hard to claim that they constituted a sufficient basis for the well-lived life. So what precisely is it that we find lacking in unrestrained financial capitalism, or 'commercial society' as the 18th century had it? What do we find instinctively amiss in our present arrangements and what can we do about them? What is it that offends our sense of propriety when faced with unfettered lobbying by the wealthy at the expense of everyone else? What have we lost?

We are all children of the Greeks. We intuitively grasp the need for a sense of moral direction: it is not necessary to be familiar with Socrates to feel that the unexamined life is not worth much. Natural Aristotelians, we assume that a just society is one in which justice is habitually practiced; a good society one in which people behave well. But in order for such an implicitly circular account to convince, we need to agree on the meaning of 'just' or 'well'.

For Aristotle and his successors, the substance of justice or goodness was as much a function of convention as of definition. Like pornography, these attributes might be impossible to define but you knew them when you saw them. The attractions of a 'reasonable' level of wealth, an 'acceptable' compromise, a just or good resolution were self-evident. The avoidance of extremes was a moral virtue in its own right, as well as a condition of political stability. However, the idea of moderation—so familiar to generations of moralists—is difficult to articulate today. Big is not always better, more not always desirable; but we are discouraged from expressing the thought.

One source of our confusion may be a blurring of the distinction between law and justice. In the US especially, so long as a practice is not illegal we find it hard to define its shortcomings. The notion of 'prudence' eludes us: the idea that it is *imprudent* as well as improper for Goldman Sachs to distribute billions of dollars in bonuses less than a year after benefiting from taxpayer largesse would have been self-evident to men of the Scottish Enlightenment, just as it would to the classical philosophers. 'Imprudence' in this respect would have been as reprehensible as financial chicanery: not least for the risks to which it exposed the community at large.

It was the distinctive achievement of the Enlightenment to weld classical moral categories to a secularized vision of human improvement: in a well-ordered society, men would not just live well but strive to live better than in the past. The idea of progress entered the ethical lexicon and dominated it for much of the ensuing two centuries. We hear echoes of this innocent optimism even today, when Americans speak enthusiastically of 'reinventing' themselves. But with the exception of the hard sciences, is 'progress' still a credible account of the world we inhabit?

The Enlightenment vision—with or without God as its first mover and moral arbiter—no longer convinces: we need reasons to choose one policy or set of policies over another. What we lack is a moral narrative: an internally coherent account that ascribes purpose to our actions in a way that transcends them. But what of the view that politics is the art of the possible and morality is something, in the words of the former British Prime Minister Harold Macmillan, best left to Archbishops? Are not all normative propositions—if taken seriously—potentially intolerant? Don't we have to start from what we have, rather than from abstract first principles?

Collective purposes may contain competing objectives. Indeed, any truly open society will want to embrace them: freedom and equality are the most obvious—and we are all by now familiar with the tension between wealth creation and environmental protection. Some sort of mutual restraint will be required if we are to take seriously all of our desires: this is a truism for any consensual system. But it speaks volumes to the degradation of public life that it sounds so idealistic today.

Idealistic and naïve: who now believes in such shared ideals? But someone has to take responsibility for what Jan Patočka called the 'Soul of the City'. It cannot indefinitely be substituted with a story of endless economic growth. Abundance (as Daniel Bell once observed) is the American substitute for socialism. But is that the best we can do?

WHAT DO WE WANT?

"My aim in life is to make life pleasanter for this great majority; I do not care if it becomes in the process less pleasant for the well to do minority."

—JOSEPH CHAMBERLAIN

Of all the competing and only partially reconcilable ends that we might seek, the reduction of inequality must come first. Under conditions of endemic inequality, all other desirable goals become hard to achieve. Whether in Delhi or Detroit, the poor and the permanently underprivileged cannot expect justice. They cannot secure medical treatment and their lives are accordingly reduced in length and potential. They cannot get a good education, and without that they cannot hope for even minimally secure employment—much less participation in the culture and civilization of their society.

In this sense, unequal access to resources of every sort—from rights to water—is the starting point of any truly progressive critique of the world. But inequality is not just a technical problem. It illustrates and exacerbates the loss of social cohesion—the sense of living in a series of gated communities whose chief purpose is to keep out other people (less fortunate than ourselves) and confine our advantages to ourselves and our families: the pathology of the age and the greatest threat to the health of any democracy.

If we remain grotesquely unequal, we shall lose all sense of fraternity: and fraternity, for all its fatuity as a political objective, turns out to be the necessary condition of politics itself. The inculcation of a sense of common purpose and mutual dependence has long been regarded as the linchpin of any community. Acting together for a common purpose is the source of enormous satisfaction, in everything from amateur sports to professional armies. In this sense, we have always known that inequality is not just morally troubling: it is *inefficient*.

The corrosive consequences of envy and resentment that arise in visibly unequal societies would be significantly mitigated under more equal conditions: the prison population of egalitarian countries bears witness to this likelihood. A less stratified population is also a better educated one: increasing opportunity for those at the bottom does nothing to reduce the prospects for those already well-placed. And better educated populations not only lead better lives, they adapt faster and at less cost to disruptive technical change.

There is quite a lot of evidence that even those who do well in unequal societies would be happier if the gap separating them from the majority of their fellow citizens were significantly reduced. They would certainly be more secure. But there is more to it than mere self-interest: living in close proximity to people whose condition constitutes a standing ethical rebuke is a source of discomfort even for the wealthy.

Selfishness is uncomfortable even for the selfish. Hence the rise of gated communities: the privileged don't like to be reminded of their privileges—if these carry morally dubious connotations. To be sure, it might be argued that after three decades of inculcated self-regard, young people in the United States and elsewhere are now immune to such sensitivities. But I do not believe this is the case. The perennial desire of youth to do something 'useful' or 'good' speaks to an instinct that we have not succeeded in repressing. Not, however, for lack of trying: why else have universities seen fit to establish 'business schools' for undergraduates?

The time has come to reverse this trend. In post-religious societies like our own, where most people find meaning and satisfaction in secular objectives, it is only by indulging what Adam Smith called our 'benevolent instincts' and reversing our selfish desires that we can ". . . produce among mankind that harmony of sentiments and passions in which consists their whole race and propriety."[29]

29 Adam Smith, *op. cit.,* p. 20.

CHAPTER SIX

The Shape of Things to Come

*"The success of postwar democracy rests
on the equilibrium between production
and redistribution, regulated by the state.
With globalization, this equilibrium is
broken. Capital has become mobile:
production has moved beyond national
borders, and thus outside the remit of
state redistribution . . . Growth would
oppose redistribution; the virtuous circle
would become the vicious circle."*

—Dominique Strauss-Kahn

In the famous opening paragraph of his *18th Brumaire of Louis Bonaparte*, Karl Marx observes that all facts and personages of importance in world history occur twice: the first time as tragedy, the second as farce. There is much to be said for this view, but it does not exclude the possibility that even tragedies may repeat themselves. Western commentators who celebrated the defeat of Communism confidently anticipated an era of peace and freedom. We should have known better.

GLOBALIZATION

"It is in the nature of things, that a state which subsists upon a revenue furnished by other countries must be infinitely more exposed to all the accidents of time and chance than one which produces its own."

—THOMAS MALTHUS

E ven economies have histories. The last great era of internationalization—'globalization' *avant le mot*—took place in the imperial decades preceding World War I. It was broadly assumed at the time, much as it is today, that 'we' (Great Britain, Western Europe, the United States) were poised on the threshold of an unprecedented age of growth and stability. International war appeared quite literally unthinkable. Not only did the great powers have every interest in the preservation of peace; war, after decades of industrialization and great advances in armaments technology, would be unspeakably destructive and intolerably expensive. No rational state or politician could possibly desire it.

Moreover, by 1914—thanks to new forms of communication, transport and exchange –the petty national quarrels and boundary disputes of empires and aspirant nations appeared absurd and anachronistic. It made no economic sense to speak of breaking up the Austrian Empire, for example: with its industrial heartland in Bohemia, its capital in Vienna and its labor force drawing on immigrants from all over central and southeastern Europe, the Empire was living evidence of the internationalization of modern economic life. No one, surely, would wish to impoverish all the constituent parts of such a natural unit merely in the name of nationalist dogma. International markets had displaced the nation-state as the primary units of human activity.

Anyone seeking an account of the tremendous self-confidence of the men of pre-1914 Europe can do no better than read Keynes's *Economic Consequences of the Peace*: a summary of the illusions of a world on the edge of catastrophe, written in the aftermath of the war that was to put an end to all such irenic fancies for the next fifty years. As Keynes reminds us, ". . . the internationalisation [of social and economic life] was nearly complete in practice."[30] To invoke a term not yet in use, the world seemed flat.

This precedent should make us cautious. The first age of globalization came to a shuddering halt. Thanks to the Great War and its aftermath, economic growth in Europe would not recover its 1913 levels until well into the 1950s. The apparently unstoppable logic of economics was trumped by the rise of new nation-states, mutually antagonistic and politically unstable. Great empires—the Russian, the Austrian, the Turkish, the German and eventually the British—all collapsed. Only the United States stood to gain from this international cataclysm: and even the US did not profit from its newfound hegemony until nearly thirty years after the end of the war that brought it about.

The optimism of the Edwardians was replaced by an enduring and gnawing insecurity. The gap between the illusions of the Gilded Age and the realities of the next four decades was filled by economic retrenchment, political demagogy and unbroken international conflict. By 1945, there was a universal "craving for security" (Keynes), addressed by the provision of public services and social safety nets incorporated into postwar systems of governance from Washington to Prague. The very term "social

30 John Maynard Keynes, *The Economic Consequences of the Peace*, in *The End of Laissez-Faire and the Economic Consequences of the Peace* (Amherst, NY: Prometheus Books, 2004), p. 62.

security"—adapted by Keynes from its new American usage—became a universal shorthand for prophylactic institutions designed to avert any return to the interwar catastrophe.

Today, it is as though the 20th century never happened. We have been swept up into a new master narrative of "integrated global capitalism", economic growth and indefinite productivity gains. Like earlier narratives of endless improvement, the story of globalization combines an evaluative mantra ("growth is good") with the presumption of inevitability: globalization is with us to stay, a natural process rather than a human choice. The ineluctable dynamic of global economic competition and integration has become the illusion of the age. As Margaret Thatcher once put it: There Is No Alternative.

We should be wary of such claims. 'Globalization' is an updating of the high modernist faith in technology and rational management which marked the enthusiasms of the postwar decades. Like them, it implicitly excludes politics as an arena of choice: systems of economic relationships are, as the 18th century physiocrats used to assert, laid down by nature. Once they have been identified and correctly understood, it remains to us only to live according to their laws.

However, it is not true that an increasingly globalized economy tends to the equalization of wealth—a defense of globalization offered by its more liberal admirers. While inequalities do indeed become less marked *between* countries, disparities of wealth and poverty *within* countries actually increased. Moreover, sustained economic expansion in itself guarantees neither equality nor prosperity; it is not even a reliable source of economic development.

After decades of rapid growth, India's per capita GDP in 2006 ($728) remained only slightly above that of sub-Saharan Africa, while on the UN Human Development Index—an aggregate calculus of social and economic indicators—the country ranked some seventy places below Cuba and Mexico, not to speak of fully developed economies. As for modernization: despite its enthusiastic and much-touted participation in the globalized economy of high technology industry and services, just 1.3 million of India's 400 million workers had jobs in the 'new economy'. To say the least, the benefits of globalization take an extraordinarily long time to trickle down.[31]

Moreover, we have no good reason to suppose that economic globalization translates smoothly into political freedom. The opening up of China and other Asian economies has merely shifted industrial production from high wage to low wage regions. Furthermore, China (like many other developing countries) is not just a low wage country—it is also and above all a

---

31 Pankaj Mishra, "Myth of the New India," *New York Times,* July 6, 2006.

'low rights' country. And it is the absence of rights which keeps wages down and will continue to do so for some time— meanwhile depressing the rights of workers in countries with which China competes. Chinese capitalism, far from liberalizing the condition of the masses, further contributes to their repression.

As to the delusion that globalization will undercut governments, facilitating the rise of corporatist market states where massive international corporations dominate international economic policy-making: the crisis of 2008 revealed this for a mirage. When banks fail, when unemployment rises dramatically, when large-scale corrective action is called for, there is no 'corporatist market state'. There is just the state as we have known it since the 18th century. That is all we have.

After decades of relative eclipse, nation-states are poised to reassert their dominant role in international affairs. Populations experiencing increased economic and physical insecurity will retreat to the political symbols, legal resources, and physical barriers that only a territorial state can provide. This is already happening in many countries: note the rising attraction of protectionism in American politics, the appeal of "anti-immigrant" parties across Western Europe, the ubiquitous calls for 'walls', 'barriers', and 'tests'.

International capital flows continue to elude domestic political regulation. But wages, hours, pensions and everything that matters to the working population of a country are still negotiated—and contested—locally. With the strains born of globalization and its attendant crises, the state will be called upon with mounting insistence to resolve the tensions that result. As the only institution standing between individuals and non-state actors like banks or international corporations; as the sole regulatory unit occupying the space between transnational agencies and local interests, the territorial state is likely to grow in political significance. It is revealing that in Germany, Angela Merkel's Christian Democrats have quietly retreated from their brief market enthusiasms to a popular identification with the social market state as an insurance against the excesses of globalized finance.

This may appear counterintuitive. Surely the promise of globalization—and more generally, of the internationalization of laws and regulations over the past half century—lay in the prospect of *transcending* the conventional state? We were supposed to be moving towards a cooperative trans-state era in which the conflicts inherent in territorially-defined political units would be consigned to history.

But just as the intermediate institutions of society—political parties, trade unions, constitutions and laws—impeded the powers of kings and tyrants, so the state itself may now be the primary 'intermediate institution': standing between powerless, insecure citizens and unresponsive, unaccountable corporations or international agencies. And the state—or at least the democratic state—retains a unique legitimacy in the eyes of its citizens. It alone answers to them, and they to it.

None of this would matter very much if the contradictions of globalization were merely passing: if we were living in a transitional moment between the twilight years of the nation-state and the new dawn of global governance. But are we so sure that globalization is here to stay? That economic internationalization carries in its wake the eclipse of national politics? It would not be the first time that we made a mistake on this count. We should by now have learned that politics remains national, even if economics does not: the history of the 20th century offers copious evidence that even in healthy democracies, bad political choices usually trump 'rational' economic calculations.

Thinking the State

"The important thing for Government is not to do things which individuals are doing already, and to do them a little better or a little worse; but to do those things which at present are not done at all."

—John Maynard Keynes

If we are indeed going to witness a return of the state, an enhanced need for the security and resources that only a government can provide, then we should be paying greater attention to the things states can do. The success of the mixed economies of the past half century has led a younger generation to take stability for granted and demand the elimination of the "impediment" of the taxing, regulating, and generally interfering state. This discounting of the public sector has become the default political language in much of the developed world.

But only a government can respond on the requisite scale to the dilemmas posed by globalized competition. These are not challenges that can be grasped, much less addressed and resolved, by any one private employer or industry. The most that can be expected of the private sector is short-term lobbying in defense of particular jobs or protection for favored sectors—a recipe for just those pathologies and inefficiencies normally associated with public ownership.

Late-Victorian reformers and their 20th century liberal successors turned to the state to address the shortcomings of the market. What could not be expected to happen 'naturally'— quite the contrary, since it was the natural workings of the market that created the 'social question' in the first place—would have to be planned, administered and, if necessary, enforced from above.

We face a similar dilemma today. Having reduced the scale of public ownership and intervention over the course of the past thirty years, we now find ourselves embracing *de facto* state action on a scale last seen in the Depression. The reaction against unrestrained financial markets—and the grotesquely disproportionate gains of a few contrasted with the losses of so many— has obliged the state to step in everywhere. But since 1989 we have been congratulating ourselves on the final defeat of the over-mighty state and are thus ill-positioned to explain to ourselves just why we need intervention and to what end.

We need to learn to *think* the state again. After all, it has always been with us. In the United States of America, the country most given to disparaging the role of government in the affairs of men, Washington has supported and even subsidized selected market actors: railway barons, wheat farmers, car manufacturers, the aircraft industry, steel works and others besides. Whatever Americans fondly believe, their government has always had its fingers in the economic pie. What distinguishes the USA from every other developed country has been the widespread belief to the contrary.

Instead, the state has been vilified as the source of economic dysfunction. By the 1990s, this rhetorical trope was widely imitated in Ireland, Poland and parts of Latin America, as well as the United Kingdom: conventional opinion was for confining the public sector, wherever possible, to administrative and security functions. In a delicious irony, the ideological enemies of the state, from Margaret Thatcher to the contemporary Republican Party, thus effectively adopted the view of Sidney Webb, the founder of Fabian Socialism, who never tired of asserting that "[t]he future belong[s] to the great administrative nations, where the officials govern and the police keep order."

How, in the face of this powerful negative myth, are we to describe the proper role of the state? We should begin by acknowledging, more than the Left has been disposed to concede, the real harm that was done and could still be done by overmighty sovereigns. There are two legitimate concerns.

Coercion is the first. Political freedom does not primarily consist in being left alone by the state: no modern administration can or should ignore its subjects altogether. Freedom, rather, consists in retaining our right to disagree with the state's purposes and express our own objections and goals without fear of retribution. This is more complicated than it may sound: even well-intentioned states and governments may not be pleased to encounter firms, communities or individuals recalcitrant in the face of majority desires. Efficiency should not be adduced to justify gross inequality; nor may it be invoked to suppress dissent in the name of social justice. It is better to be free than to live in an efficient state of any political colour if efficiency comes at such a price.

The second objection to activist states is that they can get things wrong. And when the state errs, it is likely to do so on a dramatic scale: the history of English secondary education since the 1960s is a case in point. The American sociologist James Scott has written wisely of the benefits of what he calls 'local knowledge'. The more variegated and complicated a society, the greater the chance that those at the top will be ignorant of the realities at the bottom. There are limits, he writes, ". . . in principle of what we are likely to know about a complex functioning order."[32] The benefits of state intervention on the public behalf must always be weighed against this simple truth.

This objection is different from that of Hayek and his Aus-

32 James C. Scott, *Seeing Like a State* (New Haven, CT: Yale University Press, 1998), p. 7.

trian colleagues, who opposed all top-down planning on general principles. But planning may or may not be the most efficient means to achieve economic objectives: the benefits of public action must be weighed against the risks of suppressing individual knowledge and initiative. The answers will vary by circumstance and should not be dogmatically pre-ordained.

We have freed ourselves of the mid-20th century assumption—never universal but certainly widespread—that the state is likely to be the *best* solution to any given problem. We now need to liberate ourselves from the opposite notion: that the state is—by definition and always—the *worst* available option.

The idea that there are certain areas in which the state not only may but *should* intervene was by no means anathema to conservatives: Hayek himself saw no incompatibility between economic competition (by which he meant the market) and "... an extensive system of social services—so long as the organization of these services is not designed in such a way as to make competition ineffective over wide fields."[33]

But just what is it about state services that, if poorly designed, renders competition 'ineffective'? There is no general answer: it depends on the service in question and on just how

33 Friedrich Hayek, *op. cit.,* p. 87.

effective we require competition to be. Michael Oakeshott, who regarded inefficient or distorted competition as the worst of all possible outcomes, proposed that "[u]ndertakings in which competition cannot be made to work as the agency of control must be transferred to public operation."[34] The place of the state in economic life was an essentially pragmatic question.

Keynes, characteristically, went further. The chief task of economists, he wrote in 1926, is ". . . to distinguish afresh the *Agenda* of Government from the *Non-Agenda* . . ."[35] Obviously the agenda in question varies with the politics of those pursuing it. Liberals might confine themselves to the alleviation of poverty, extreme inequality and disadvantage. Conservatives would restrict the agenda to legislation favoring a well-regulated competitive market. But that the state needs an agenda and a way of carrying it out is uncontentious.

What, then, of the contemporary belief that we can either have benevolent social service states or efficient, growth-generating free markets but not both? On this, Karl Popper, Hayek's fellow Austrian, had something to say: "[a] free market is paradoxical. If the state does not interfere, then other semi-political organizations, such as monopolies, trusts, unions, etc.

---

34 Michael Oakeshott, *op. cit.,* p. 405.
35 Keynes, *The End of Laissez-Faire,* p. 37.

may interfere, reducing the freedom of the market to a fiction."[36] This paradox is crucial. The market is always at risk of being distorted by over-mighty participants, whose behavior eventually constrains the government to interfere in order to protect its workings.

The market, over time, is its own worst enemy. Indeed, the valiant and ultimately successful efforts of New Dealers to set American capitalism back on its feet were most vigorously opposed by many of their eventual beneficiaries. But although market failure may be catastrophic, market *success* is just as politically dangerous. The task of the state is not just to pick up the pieces when an under-regulated economy bursts. It is also to contain the effects of immoderate gains. After all, many Western industrial countries were doing extraordinarily well in the era of Edwardian social reform: in the aggregate, they were growing fast and wealth was multiplying. But the proceeds were ill-distributed and it was this more than anything which led to calls for reform and regulation.

There are things that the state can accomplish that no one person or group could do alone. Thus while a man can build a path around his garden by his own efforts, he can hardly build a freeway to the next city—nor would he go to the expense of

---

36 Quoted in Malachi Hacohen, *op. cit.*, p. 502.

doing so, since he would never recoup the benefits. This is not news. It will be familiar to readers of Adam Smith's *Wealth of Nations*, where he writes that there are certain public institutions a society needs and of which ". . . the profit could never repay the expense to any individual or small number of individuals".[37]

Even the most altruistic among us cannot act alone. Nor can we pursue public goods by voluntary association: 'faith-based initiatives'. Suppose that a group of people got together and agreed to build and maintain a playing field, for their own use above all but in the middle of their village and open to everyone. Even if these great-hearted volunteers could raise among themselves sufficient funds to do the work, problems arise.

How do they keep other people—free riders—from benefiting from their efforts without making any contribution? By fencing the field and keeping it exclusively for their own use? By charging others a fee to rent it? But in that case the field becomes private. Public goods—if they are to remain public—need to be provided at public expense. Could the market do the job better? Why should someone not build a private playing field and charge for it? With enough takers, he could reduce his fees to the point where almost everyone could afford to

37 Quoted in Emma Rothschild, *op. cit.,* p. 239.

benefit from the facility. The problem here is that the market cannot cater to every case of what economists call 'option demand': the amount that any one individual would be willing to pay to have a facility to hand for those infrequent occasions when he wants to use it.

We would all like a nice playing field in our village, just as we would all like a good rail service to the nearest town, a range of shops carrying the goods we need, a conveniently-sited post office and so forth. But the only way we can be made to pay for such things—including the free riders among us—is by general taxation. No one has come up with a better way of aggregating individual desires to collective advantage.

It would seem to follow that the 'invisible hand' is not much help when it comes to practical legislation. There are too many areas of life where we cannot be relied upon to advance our collective interests merely by doing what we think is best for each of us. Today, when the market and the free play of private interests so obviously do *not* come together to collective advantage, we need to know when to intervene.

RAILROADS: A CASE STUDY

> *"[R]ailway stations . . . do not constitute, so to*
> *speak, a part of the surrounding town but contain*
> *the essence of its personality just as upon their*
> *signboards they bear its painted name."*

> —MARCEL PROUST

I magine a classic railway station: Waterloo Station in London, for example, or the Gare de l'Est in Paris—Mumbai's dramatic Victoria Terminus, or Berlin's magnificent new Hauptbahnhof. In these cathedrals of modern life, the private sector has its place: there is no reason why newsstands or coffee bars should be run by the state. Anyone who can recall the desiccated, plastic-wrapped sandwiches of British Railway's cafés will readily concede that competition in this arena is to be encouraged.

But you cannot run trains competitively. Railways—like agriculture or the mails—are at one and the same time an economic activity and an essential public good. Moreover, you cannot render a railway system more efficient by placing two trains on a track and waiting to see which performs better, like two brands of butter on a supermarket shelf. Passengers do not choose which of two simultaneous trains to board, based on appearance, comfort or price. They take the train that comes. Railways are a natural monopoly.

This is not to say that railways cannot be privatized. They have been in many places. But the consequences are usually perverse. Let us suppose that the government authorized Safeway to exercise a five-year monopoly on supermarket sales for the region extending from Boston to Providence, or London to Bristol. Allow further that the government guaranteed Safeway against a loss on its business. Finally, Safeway are issued with copious written instructions on what to sell, the price range within which they could sell it and the times and days when they were to be open for business.

Obviously, no self-respecting supermarket chain would take up the offer—nor would any sane politician make it. But these, in effect, are the terms under which private companies have been operating trains in the UK since the mid-1990s: combining the very worst of monopolistic market control, state interference and moral hazard. The reason we find the supermarket analogy absurd, of course, is that competition among grocery stores makes good economic sense. But competition among rail companies along one set of existing tracks is simply not possible. In that case, the monopoly should be maintained in public hands.

Arguments from efficiency, conventionally invoked to justify private enterprise over public service, do not apply in the case of public transportation. The paradox of public transport is quite simply that the better it does its job, the less 'efficient' it may be. Thus, a private company that offers an express bus service for those who can afford it and avoids remote villages where it would be boarded only by the occasional pensioner will make more money for its owner. In this sense it is efficient. But someone—the state or the local municipality—must still provide the unprofitable, 'inefficient' local service to those pensioners.

In the absence of such a service, there may certainly be short-term economic benefits. But these will be offset by long-term damage to the community at large—difficult to quantify but unquestionably real: the example of privatization in British bus services may be taken as a case in point. Predictably, the consequences of 'competitive' buses—except in London, where there is a superfluity of demand—have been a reduction in services; an increase in costs assigned to the public sector; a sharp rise in fares to the level that the market can bear—and attractive profits for the express bus companies.

Trains, like buses, are above all a *social* service. Almost anyone could run a profitable rail line if all they had to do was shunt busy expresses back and forth from London to Edinburgh, Paris to Marseilles, Boston to Washington. But what of rail links to and from places where people take the train only occasionally?

No single person is going to set aside sufficient funds to pay the economic cost of supporting such a service for the rare moments when she uses it. Only the collectivity—the state, the government, the local authorities—can do this. The subsidy required will always appear inefficient in the eyes of a certain sort of economist: would it not be cheaper to rip up the tracks and let everyone use their car?

In 1996, the last year before Britain's railways were privatized, British Rail boasted the lowest public subsidy for a railway in Europe. In that year the French were planning for their railways an investment rate of £21 per head of population; the Italians £33; the British just £9. Moreover, in those same years the UK Treasury was demanding a 10% return on its investment in the electrification of England's East Coast Main Line—a far higher rate than was mandated for freeway construction. These contrasts were accurately reflected in the quality of the service provided by the respective national systems.

They also explain why the British rail network could be privatized only at great loss, so shoddy was its infrastructure: very few buyers were willing to take the risk except when offered expensive guarantees. The parsimonious investments of the British Treasury in its nationalized rail network—or of the US administration in state-owned Amtrak—suggest (correctly) that state ownership per se is no guarantee of a well-managed transportation system. Conversely, while some traditionally private rail systems are well-financed and provide (indeed, are required to provide) a first-rate public service—the regional railways of Switzerland come to mind—most do not.

The investment contrast between the US and the UK on the one hand and most of continental Europe on the other illustrates my point. The French and the Italians have long treated their railways as a *social* provision. Running a train to a remote region, however cost-ineffective, sustains local communities. It reduces environmental damage by offering an alternative to road transport. The railway station and the facilities it provides to even the smallest of communities are both a symptom and a symbol of society as a shared aspiration.

I suggested above that the provision of train service to remote districts makes social sense even if it is economically 'inefficient'. But this, of course, begs an important question. What precisely constitutes efficiency and inefficiency in the provision of a public service? Cost is clearly one factor—we cannot simply print money to pay for all the public goods we desire. Even the most irenic social democrat must accept the need to make choices. But there is more than one kind of cost to be considered when deciding among competing priorities: there are opportunity costs too—the things we lose by making the wrong decision.

In the early 1960s, the British government adopted the recommendations of a committee chaired by Dr. Richard Beeching and closed down 34% of the country's railway network—in the name of savings and efficiency. Forty years later we can assess the true price of this catastrophic decision: the environmental costs of building freeways and encouraging car usage; the harm done to thousands of towns and villages deprived of efficient links to each other and the rest of the country; the vast expense entailed in rebuilding, renovating or re-opening defunct lines and routes many decades later when their value was once again appreciated. So just how efficient were Dr. Beeching's recommendations?

The only way to avoid such mistakes in the future is to re-think the criteria we employ to assess costs of all kinds: social, environmental, human, aesthetic and cultural as well as economic. This is where the example of public transportation in general and railroads in particular has something important to teach us. Public transport is not just another service, and trains are not just another way to convey people from point A to point B. Their emergence in the early-19th century coincided with the emergence of modern society and the service state; their respective fates are closely interwoven.

Ever since the invention of trains, travel has been the symbol and symptom of modernity: trains—along with bicycles, motorcycles, buses, cars and airplanes—have been invoked in art and commerce as proof of a society's presence at the cutting edge. In most cases, however, the invocation of a particular form of transport as the emblem of novelty and contemporaneity was ephemeral. Bicycles were 'new' just once, in the 1890s. Motor bikes were 'new' in the 1920s, for Fascists and Bright Young Things (ever since they have been evocatively 'retro'). Cars (like planes) were 'new' in the Edwardian decade and again, briefly, in the 1950s; since then they have stood for many things—reliability, prosperity, conspicuous consumption, freedom: but not 'modernity' per se.

Railways are different. Trains were already the symbol of modern life by the 1840s—hence their appeal to 'modernist' painters from Turner to Monet. They were still performing that role in the age of the great cross-country expresses of the 1890s. Electrified tube trains were the idols of modernist poets and graphic artists after 1900; nothing was more ultra-modern than the new, streamlined super-liners that graced the neo-expressionist posters of the 1930s. The Japanese Shinkansen and French TGV are the very icons of technological wizardry and high comfort at 190 mph today.

Trains, it would seem, are perennially contemporary—even if they slip from sight for a while: in this sense, any country without an efficient rail network is in crucial respects 'backwards'. Much the same applies to railway stations. The gas 'station' [sic] of the early trunk road is an object of nostalgic affection when depicted or remembered today, but it has been serially replaced by functionally updated variations and its original form survives only in fond recall. Airports typically (and irritatingly) linger well past the onset of aesthetic or functional obsolescence; but no one would wish to preserve them for their own sake, much less suppose that an airport built in 1930 or even 1960 could be of use or interest today.

But railway stations built a century or even a century and a half ago—Paris's Gare De l'Est (1852), Paddington Station, London (1854), Budapest's Keleti pályaudvar (1884), Zurich's Hauptbahnhof (1893)—not only inspire affection: they are aesthetically appealing and they *work*. More to the point, they work in the same way that they did when they were first built. This is a testament to the quality of their design and construction, of course; but it also speaks to their perennial relevance. They do not 'date'.

Stations are not an adjunct to modern life, or part of it, or a by-product of it. Like the railway they punctuate, stations are integral to the modern world itself. The topography and daily life of cities from Milan to Mumbai would be unimaginably altered if their great railway termini suddenly disappeared. London would be unthinkable (and unlivable) without its

Underground—which is why the humiliatingly unsuccessful attempts of the New Labour governments to privatize the Tube tell us so much about their attitude to the modern state at large. New York's very lifeblood flows through its ramshackle but indispensable subway network.

We too readily assume that the defining feature of modernity is the individual: the non-reducible subject, the freestanding person, the unbound self, the un-beholden citizen. This unattached individual is favourably contrasted with the dependent and deferential subject of the pre-modern world. There is something to this account: 'individualism' may be the cant of our time but for good and ill it speaks to the connected isolation of the wireless age. However, what is truly distinctive about modern life is not the unattached individual. It is society. More precisely civil—or (as the 19th century had it) bourgeois—society.

Railways remain the necessary and natural accompaniment to the emergence of civil society. They are a collective project for individual benefit. They cannot exist without common accord and, in recent times, common expenditure: by design they offer a practical benefit to individual and collectivity alike. This is something neither the market nor globalization can accomplish—except by happy inadvertence. Railways were not always environmentally sensitive—though in overall pollution costs the steam engine did less harm than its internally-combusted competitor—but from their earliest days, they were and had to be socially responsive. That is one reason why they were not very profitable.

If we abandon the railways, or hand them over to the private sector and evade collective responsibility for their fate, we shall have lost a valuable practical asset whose replacement or recovery would be intolerably expensive. If we throw away the railway stations—as we began to do in the 1950s and '60s, with the vandalous destruction of Euston Station, Gare Montparnasse and, above all, the great Pennsylvania Railroad Station in Manhattan—we shall be throwing away our memory of how to live the confident civic life. It is not by chance that Margaret Thatcher made a point of never travelling by train.

If we cannot see the case for expending our collective resources on trains, it will not just be because we have all joined gated communities and no longer need anything but private cars to move around between them. It will be because we have become gated individuals who do not know how to share public space to common advantage. The implications of such a loss would far transcend the decline or demise of one system of transport among others. It would mean we had done with modern life itself.

THE POLITICS OF FEAR

"The alleged clash between freedom and security . . . turns out to be a chimera. For there is no freedom if it is not secured by the state; and conversely, only a state which is controlled by the free citizens can offer them any reasonable security."

—KARL POPPER

The case for reviving the state does not rest uniquely upon its contributions to modern society as a collective project; there is a more urgent consideration. We have entered an age of fear. Insecurity is once again an active ingredient of political life in Western democracies. Insecurity born of terrorism, of course; but also, and more insidiously, fear of the uncontrollable speed of change, fear of the loss of employment, fear of losing ground to others in an increasingly unequal distribution of resources, fear of losing control of the circumstances and routines of our daily life. And, perhaps above all, fear that it is not just *we* who can no longer shape our lives but that those in authority have also lost control, to forces beyond their reach.

We in the West have lived through a long era of stability, cocooned in the illusion of indefinite economic improvement.

But all that is now behind us. For the foreseeable future we shall be deeply economically insecure. We are assuredly less confident of our collective purposes, our environmental well-being, or our personal safety than at any time since World War II. We have no idea what sort of world our children will inherit, but we can no longer delude ourselves into supposing that it must resemble our own.

The best reason for hoping that we shall not recycle the errors of the 1930s is that we have been there before. However inadequately we recall the past, it is unlikely that we shall neglect *all* the lessons that it has taught. More plausibly, we shall make unprecedented mistakes of our own—with perverse political consequences. Indeed, it is probably good fortune rather than wise judgment that has preserved us from the latter so far. But we would be ill-advised to rest on such laurels.

In 2008, 43% of American voters favored the election of Sarah Palin to the Vice Presidency of the United States—a heart-beat away from what is still the most powerful political office in the world. Like Dutch demagogues playing on local fears of Muslim immigrants or French politicians exploiting anxieties over the dilution of French 'identity', Palin and her ilk can only benefit from rising confusion and anxiety in the face of apparently unmanageable change.

Familiarity reduces insecurity, so we feel more comfortable

describing and combating the risks we think we understand: terrorists, immigrants, job loss or crime. But the true sources of insecurity in decades to come will be those that most of us cannot define: dramatic climate change and its social and environmental effects; imperial decline and its attendant 'small wars'; collective political impotence in the face of distant upheavals with disruptive local impact. These are the threats that chauvinist politicians will be best placed to exploit, precisely because they lead so readily to anger and humiliation.

The more exposed the society, the weaker the state and the greater the misplaced faith in 'the market', the higher the likelihood of a political backlash. In former Communist countries, a generation has been raised to believe in the free market and the minimal state: not just as ends in themselves, but as the opposite of everything that was wrong with the old regime. Where 'klepto-capitalism' has succeeded corrupt socialist regimes with alarming transitional ease, surviving an age of unprecedented insecurity is likely to pose a difficult challenge to fragile democratic structures.

Young people in eastern Europe have been led to suppose that economic freedom and the interventionist state are mutually exclusive—a dogma they share with the American Republican Party. Ironically, this echoes the Communists' own view of the matter: a retreat to authoritarianism may thus prove seductive in countries where that tradition retains considerable subterranean support.

North Americans and western Europeans fondly suppose that there is a necessary relationship between democracy, rights, liberalism and economic progress. But for most people, most of the time, the legitimacy and credibility of a political system rests not on liberal practices or democratic forms but upon order and predictability. A stable authoritarian regime is a lot more desirable for most of its citizens than a failed democratic state. Even justice probably counts for less than administrative competence and order in the streets. If we can have democracy, we will. But above all, we want to be safe. As global threats mount, so the attractions of order will only grow.

The implications for even the best-established democracies are significant. In the absence of strong institutions of communal trust, or reliable services furnished by a properly funded public sector, men and women will seek out private substitutes. Religion—as faith, community and doctrine—is likely to undergo a measure of revival even in the secular West. Outsiders, however defined, will be seen as threats, foes and challenges. As in the past, the promise of stability risks merging with the comforts of protection. Unless the Left has something better to offer, we should not be surprised to find voters responding to those holding out such promises.

We must revisit the ways in which our grandparents' generation handled comparable challenges and threats. Social democracy in Europe, the New Deal and the Great Society here in the US, were explicit responses to them. Few in the West today can conceive of a complete breakdown of liberal institutions, an utter disintegration of the democratic consensus. But what we know of World War II—or the former Yugoslavia—illustrates the ease with which *any* society can descend into Hobbesian nightmares of unrestrained atrocity and violence. If we are going to build a better future, it must begin with a deeper appreciation of the ease with which even solidly-grounded liberal democracies can founder. To put the point quite bluntly, if social democracy has a future, it will be as a social democracy of fear.

Accordingly, the first task is to remind ourselves of the achievements of the 20th century, along with the likely consequences of a heedless rush to dismantle them. This may sound less exciting than planning great radical adventures for the future, and perhaps it is. But as the British political theorist John Dunn has wisely observed, the past is somewhat better lit than the future: we see it more clearly.

The Left has something to conserve. And why not? In one sense radicalism has always been about conserving valuable pasts. In October 1647, in the Putney Debates conducted at the height of the English Civil War, Colonel Thomas Rainsborough famously warned his interlocutors that: "[t]*he poorest he that is in England hath a life to live, as the greatest he . . . every man that is to live under a government ought first by his own consent to put himself under that government . . .*" Rainsborough was not pointing to some misty-eyed egalitarian future; he was invoking the widely held belief that the rights of Englishmen had been stolen and must be reclaimed.

In a similar way, the anger of early-19th century radicals in France and Britain was driven in very considerable measure by the belief that there were moral rules to economic life, and that these were being trampled underfoot by the new world of industrial capitalism. It is that sense of loss—and the revolutionary sentiments it stoked—which fired the political energies of early socialists. The Left has always had something to conserve.

We take for granted the institutions, legislation, services and rights that we have inherited from the great age of 20th century reform. It is time to remind ourselves that all of these were utterly inconceivable as recently as 1929. We are the fortunate beneficiaries of a transformation whose scale and impact was unprecedented. There is much to defend.

Moreover, 'defensive' Social Democracy has a very respectable heritage. In France, at the turn of the 20th century, the Socialist leader Jean Jaurès urged his colleagues to support small shopkeepers and skilled artisans driven under by the rise of department stores and mass production. Socialism in his view was not merely a forward projection into a post-capitalist future; it was also and above all a protection for the helpless and those threatened with economic extinction.

We do not typically associate 'the Left' with caution. In the political imaginary of Western culture, 'left' denotes radical, destructive and innovatory. But in truth there is a close relationship between progressive institutions and a spirit of *prudence*. The democratic Left has often been motivated by a sense of loss: sometimes of idealized pasts, sometimes of moral interests ruthlessly overridden by private advantage. It is doctrinaire market liberals who for the past two centuries have embraced the relentlessly optimistic view that all economic change is for the better.

It is the *Right* that has inherited the ambitious modernist urge to destroy and innovate in the name of a universal project. From the war in Iraq through the unrequited desire to dismantle public education and health services, to the decades-long project of financial deregulation, the political Right—from Thatcher and Reagan to Bush and Blair—has abandoned the association of political conservatism with social moderation which served it so well from Disraeli to Heath, from Theodore Roosevelt to Nelson Rockefeller.

If it is true, as Bernard Williams once observed, that the best grounds for toleration are "... the manifest evils of toleration's absence",[38] then much the same should be said of social democracy and the welfare state. It is difficult for young people to appreciate just what life was like before them. But if we cannot rise to the level of a justificatory narrative—if we lack the will to theorize our better instincts—then let us at least recall the well-documented cost of abandoning them.

Social democrats are characteristically modest—a political quality whose virtues are overestimated. We need to apologize a little less for past shortcomings and speak more assertively of achievements. That these were always incomplete should not trouble us. If we have learned nothing else from the 20th century, we should at least have grasped that the more perfect the answer, the more terrifying its consequences.

Incremental improvements upon unsatisfactory circumstances are the best that we can hope for, and probably all we should seek. Others have spent the last three decades methodically unraveling and destabilizing them: this should make us much angrier than we are. It ought also to worry us, if only on prudential grounds: why have we been in such a hurry to tear down the dikes laboriously set in place by our predecessors? Are we so sure that there are no floods to come?

To abandon the labors of a century is to betray those who

---

38   Bernard Williams, *op. cit.,* p. 134.

came before us as well as generations yet to come. It would be pleasing—but misleading—to promise that social democracy, or something like it, represents the future that we would paint for ourselves in an ideal world. But this would be to return to discredited story-telling. Social democracy does not represent an ideal future; it does not even represent the ideal past. But among the options available to us today, it is better than anything else to hand.

What Is Living and What
Is Dead in Social Democracy?

"There was much in it that I did not
understand, in some ways I did not even
like it, but I recognized it immediately
as a state of affairs worth fighting for."

—GEORGE ORWELL, *HOMAGE TO CATALONIA*

In October 2009 I delivered a lecture in New York in which I discussed some of the themes raised in this book. The first question came from a twelve year old schoolboy; I think it worth recording here, as it speaks to a concern with which I want to conclude. The questioner came directly to the point: *"Ok, so on a daily basis if you're having a conversation or even a debate about some of these issues and the word socialism is mentioned, sometimes it is as though a brick has fallen on the conversation and there's no way to return it to its form. What would you recommend as a way to restore the conversation?"*

As I noted in my response, the 'brick' falls somewhat differently in Sweden. Allusions to socialism, even today, do not produce an embarrassed silence in European discussions any more than they do in Latin America or many other parts of the world. This is a distinctively American response—and the questioner, as an American child, had a very good point. One of the challenges of shifting the direction of public policy debate in the US is to overcome the ingrained suspicion of anything that smacks of 'socialism' or can be tarred with that brush.

There are two ways to meet this challenge. The first is simply to set aside 'socialism'. We could acknowledge the extent to which the word and the idea have been polluted by their association with 20th century dictatorships and exclude it from our discussion. This has the merit of simplicity, but it invites the charge of hypocrisy. If an idea or a policy talks like socialism and walks like socialism, should we not acknowledge that this is what it is? Can we not hope to retrieve the word from the dustbin of history?

I don't think so. 'Socialism' is a 19th century idea with a 20th century history. That is not an insuperable impediment: the same might be said of liberalism. But the baggage of history is real—the Soviet Union and most of its dependencies described themselves as 'socialist' and no amount of special pleading ("it wasn't real socialism") can get around that. For the same reasons, Marxism is irretrievably sullied by its heritage, whatever the benefits we can still reap from reading Marx. To preface every radical proposal with the adjective 'socialist' is simply to invite a sterile debate.

But there is a significant distinction between 'socialism' and 'social democracy'. Socialism was about transformative change: the displacement of capitalism with a successor regime based on an entirely different system of production and ownership. Social democracy, in contrast, was a compromise: it implied the acceptance of capitalism—and parliamentary democracy—as the framework within which the hitherto neglected interests of large sections of the population would now be addressed.

These differences matter. Socialism—under all its many guises and hyphenated incarnations—has failed. Social democracy has not only come to power in many countries, it has succeeded beyond the wildest dreams of its founders. What was idealistic in the mid-19th century and a radical challenge fifty years later has become everyday politics in many liberal states.

Thus, when 'social democracy' rather than 'socialism' is introduced into a conversation in western Europe, or Canada or New Zealand, bricks do not fall. Instead, the discussion is likely to take an intensely practical and technical turn: can we still afford universal pension schemes, unemployment compensation, subsidized arts, inexpensive higher education, etc., or are these benefits and services now too costly to sustain? If so, how should they be rendered affordable? Which of them—if any—is indispensable?

The broader question, implicitly raised by their more ideologically-motivated critics, is whether such social service states *ought* to continue in their present form or whether they have outlived their usefulness. Is a system of 'cradle-to-grave' protections and guarantees more 'useful' than a market-driven society in which the role of the state is kept to the minimum?

The answer depends on what we think 'useful' means: what sort of a society do we want and what sort of arrangements are we willing to tolerate or seek in order to bring it about? As I hope I have shown in this book, the question of 'usefulness' needs to be recast. If we confine ourselves to issues of economic efficiency and productivity, ignoring ethical considerations and all reference to broader social goals, we cannot hope to engage it.

Does social democracy have a future? In the last decades of the 20th century, it became commonplace to suggest that the reason the social democratic consensus of the previous generation had begun to crumble was that it could not develop a vision—much less practical institutions—that transcended the national state. If the world was becoming smaller and states more marginal to the daily operations of the international economy, what could social democracy hope to offer?

This concern took acute form in 1981, when the last Socialist president of France was elected on the promise that he would ignore European-level regulations and agreements and inaugurate an autonomous (socialist) future for his country. Within two years, Francois Mitterrand had reversed course—much as the British Labour Party would a few years later—and accepted what now appeared inevitable: there could be no distinctively social democratic national policies (on taxation, redistribution or public ownership) if these fell foul of international agreements.

Even in Scandinavia, where social democratic institutions were far more culturally ingrained, membership of the EU—or even just participation in the World Trade Organization and other international agencies—appeared to constrain locally-initiated legislation. In short, social democracy seemed doomed by that same internationalization which its early theorists had so enthusiastically adumbrated as the future of capitalism.

From this perspective, social democracy—like liberalism—was a byproduct of the rise of the European nation-state: a political idea keyed to the social challenges of industrialization in developed societies. Not only was there no 'socialism' in America, but social democracy as a working compromise between radical goals and liberal traditions lacked widespread support in any other continent. There was no shortage of enthusiasm for *revolutionary* socialism in much of the non-Western world, but the distinctively European compromise did not export well.

In addition to being confined to one privileged continent, social democracy appeared to be the product of unique historical circumstances. Why should we suppose that these circumstances would repeat themselves? And if they do not, why would future generations necessarily follow their grandparents into the prophylactic and prudent compromises of earlier decades?

But when circumstances change, opinions should follow. We shall not soon hear again from the ideologues of free market dogma. The so-called G20 group of important countries is much resented by lesser states excluded from its deliberations, and its drive to become the decision-making center of the future carries significant risks; but the emergence of such a grouping surely confirms the return of the state to center stage. Reports of its death have been greatly exaggerated.

If we are going to have states, and if they are going to count for something in the affairs of men, then the social democratic heritage remains relevant. The past has something to teach us. Edmund Burke, in his dyspeptic contemporary critique of the French Revolution, warned against the juvenile propensity to dispense with the past in the name of the future. Society, he wrote, is ". . . a partnership not only between those who are living, but between those who are living, those who are dead and those who are to be born."

This observation is typically read as conservative. But Burke is right. *All* political arguments need to begin with an appreciation of our relationship not only to dreams of future betterment, but also to past achievements: our own and those of our predecessors. For too long, the Left has been insensitive to this requirement: we have been in thrall to the 19th century Romantics, in too much of a hurry to put the old world behind us and offer a radical critique of everything existing. Such a critique may be the necessary condition of serious change, but it can lead us dangerously astray.

For in reality, we only build on what we have. We are, as those same Romantics well knew, rooted in history. But in the 19th century, 'history' sat uncomfortably upon the shoulders of a generation impatient for change. The institutions of the past were an impediment. Today, we have good grounds for thinking differently. We owe our children a better world than we inherited; but we also owe something to those who came before.

However, social democracy cannot just be about preserving worthy institutions as a defense against worse options. Nor need it be. Much of what is amiss in our world can best be captured in the language of classical political thought: we are intuitively familiar with issues of injustice, unfairness, inequality and immorality—we have just forgotten how to talk about them. Social democracy once articulated such concerns, until it too lost its way.

In Germany, the Social Democratic Party is accused by its critics of abandoning ideals in pursuit of selfish and provincial objectives. Social democrats all across Europe are hard-pressed to say what they stand for. Protecting and defending local or sectional interests is not enough. The temptation to calculate thus, to conceive of German (or Dutch, or Swedish) social democracy as something for Germans (or Dutch or Swedes), was always present: today it seems to have triumphed.

The silence with which western European social democrats greeted the atrocities in the Balkans—a faraway region of which they preferred to remain ignorant—has not been forgotten by the victims. Social democrats need to learn once again how to think beyond their borders: there is something deeply incoherent about a radical politics grounded in aspirations to equality or social justice that is deaf to broader ethical challenges and humanitarian ideals.

George Orwell once observed that "[t]he thing that attracts ordinary men to Socialism and makes them willing to risk their skins for it, the 'mystique' of Socialism, is the idea of equality."[39] This is still the case. It is the growing *inequality* in and between societies that generates so many social pathologies. Grotesquely unequal societies are also unstable societies. They generate internal division and, sooner or later, internal strife—usually with undemocratic outcomes.

I found it particularly reassuring to learn, from my twelve year old interlocutor, that such matters are once again being discussed by schoolchildren—even if mention of 'socialism' does bring the conversation to a shuddering halt. When I began university teaching, in 1971, students spoke obsessively of socialism, revolution, class conflict and the like—usually with reference to what was then called 'the third world': nearer to home, these matters appeared largely resolved. Over the course of the next two decades, the conversation retreated to more self-referential concerns: feminism, gay rights and identity politics. Among the more politically sophisticated, there emerged an interest in human rights and the resurgent language of 'civil society'. For a brief moment around 1989, young people in western universities were drawn to liberation efforts not only in eastern Europe and China but also in Latin America and South Africa: liberty—

39 George Orwell, *Homage to Catalonia* (New York: Mariner Books, 1980, original publication 1938), p. 104.

from enslavement, coercion, repression and atrocity—was the great theme of the day.

And then came the '90s: the first of two lost decades, during which fantasies of prosperity and limitless personal advancement displaced all talk of political liberation, social justice or collective action. In the English-speaking world, the selfish amoralism of Thatcher and Reagan—"Enrichissez-vous!", in the words of the 19th century French statesman Guizot—gave way to the vacant phrase-making of baby-boom politicians. Under Clinton and Blair, the Atlantic world stagnated smugly.

Until the late '80s, it was quite uncommon to encounter promising students who expressed any interest in attending business school. Indeed, business schools themselves were largely unknown outside of North America. Today, the aspiration—and the institution—are commonplace. And in the classroom, the enthusiasm of an earlier generation for radical politics has given way to blank mystification. In 1971 almost everyone was, or wanted to be thought, some sort of a 'Marxist'. By the year 2000, few undergraduates had any idea what that even meant, much less why it was once so appealing.

So it would be pleasing to conclude with the thought that we are on the brink of a new age, and that the selfish decades lie behind us. But were my students of the 1990s and after truly selfish? Assured from all quarters that radical change lay in the past, they saw around them no examples to follow, no arguments to engage and no goals to pursue. If the purpose of life as lived by everyone you see is to succeed in business, then this will become the default goal of all but the most independent young person. As we know from Tolstoy, "[t]here are no conditions of life to which a man cannot get accustomed, especially if he sees them accepted by everyone around him."

In writing this book, I hope I have offered some guidance to those—the young especially—trying to articulate their objections to our way of life. However, this is not enough. As citizens of a free society, we have a duty to look critically at our world. But if we think we know what is wrong, we must *act* upon that knowledge. Philosophers, it was famously observed, have hitherto only interpreted the world in various ways; the point is to change it.